That Extra Scratch Behind the Ear

Renaissance Grooming

Preface

When I decided to leave the wonderful and diversified life of a human hairstylist and move on to more challenging clients, dogs and cats, I thought my Mom was going to pee her pants laughing! Back when I first got my hairdressing license, she wanted me to be her groomer and style all her champion Shelties on the show circuit and I said “No” emphatically. Mom Asked” Well why do you want to ‘do’ old ladies hair instead of dogs?” My humorous reply, “Because old ladies don’t bite!” But I did watch my Mom while she groomed her dogs and I read all her books and found that dog grooming was the same as hairstyling on humans minus the chemical treatments and the dogs and cats have more hair, four legs, teeth and a tail.

So there I sat 31 years later with all my experience working as a stylist in theatre, film, on models, in a few retirement homes, a funeral parlor doing ‘heads of hair’, wig making and two salons under my belt; I decided to swallow my pride and tell my Mom what I was up to for the last 6 months.

She asked only one question after she recovered from her fit of laughter, “How do you like styling dogs after working on humans?”

“I’ve learned to appreciate dogs more,” I replied.

This book is written with years of experience in the area of hairstyling, years of knowledge in training and retraining animals and these skills are applied to the dogs and cats that sit on my grooming table today. In my observations I’ve discovered a lot of bad grooming habits and outdated/bad grooming training techniques being learned and taught plus the struggle of the loving owner to find and secure a good groomer for their beloved pet.

This book is written to give your dog a voice and 'that extra scratch behind the ear' it deserves for their unconditional love, loyalty and patience in your search, as their owner for a quality groomer.

This book is also written to teach old and new groomers that there are better and less stressful ways to groom dogs and cats and yes you can teach 'old dogs' new tricks!

And finally, this book is written because as of now, Grooming is not regulated in Canada under the Journeyman and Apprenticeship Boards as a spinoff of the Hairstyling Trade, creating proper instruction, examination, Apprenticeship, licensing and a Standard of Ethics of Grooming on a "Living Being". I am hoping, for now, this book will help change the conditions in the grooming salons for the better and retrain the groomers for a higher quality of talent. Help me change the grooming world in Canada for the better. debbieculos@gmail.com

That Extra Scratch Behind the Ear - Chapter #1

What to Look For in a Grooming Salon/Groomer

When looking for that perfect grooming salon and groomer for your dog or cat, your five senses are always your best bet.

Sight

- Does the salon look clean? What is the expression on the receptionist like?
- How about the faces of the other groomers are they happy, frowning, tense or relaxed?
- How is the body language of the other dogs, are the tails wagging or between their legs? Are they panting or shaking, are their eyes alert and relaxed or fearful?
- Is the floor clean? Can you see hairballs rolling across the floor or in the corner? Are the windows and walls clean? Are there garbage cans within easy reach of every station?
- Does the equipment look well maintained and clean? Can you see Barbicide or possibly a sterilizer to clean equipment and blades?
- What do the bathing and drying areas look like? Is the tub clean?
- If you can, watch the groomers at work while you are waiting.
- How do they treat the dogs on their tables? How do the dogs react to the groomers?
- Are there kennels?
- Is there fresh water for the dogs?
- Do the dogs have access to a fenced yard for their business?

Smell

- How does the salon smell? Can you smell garbage, urine or stool, wet dog or clean gently fragranced air?
- How does the bathing room smell? Do you smell mould or mildew, dirty wet dogs or the light fragrance of shampoo and conditioner?

Hearing

- How do the other dogs sound, barking whining or silent with relaxed panting?
- Is the background music easy or jarring to the ears?
- The tone of voices from the receptionist and groomers, are they calm, easy going or impatient, harried or rude?

Touch

Does the salon feel clean wherever you touch, for example door handles, floors where you walk, counter tops, etc.

Gut Instinct

The most important sense is your gut instinct about the salon. If your gut screams **no way Jose,** turn around and leave, don't forget the dog.

Remember, a dog lives by these five senses (6 senses including taste) 24/7 and are finely tuned, hence their quick response to certain places and people.

Can the Owners watch?

The biggest complaint owners have about groomers is that they can't watch how the groomer works on their dog. Especially, when their spunky, happy dog shake and shivers, whines or has to be dragged to go through the salon door because they are afraid. Some dogs are so scared they defecate or urinate. The worst reaction is when the dog totally ignores the owner for days after being groomed because the dog is so upset. The owner is justifiably worried at this unusual behaviour or fear displayed by their dog because they are not normally like this.

So the owner asks the obvious question, "What happened to my dog while he was here?"

The owner received the usual and very vague replies, "Oh I think another dog scared him." Or "Your dog bit me." Or "Nothing different." Etc., etc., etc.

Some owners have hidden behind displays to observe their dog being groomed and have been appalled at what they see the groomer doing to their dog. Hitting, yelling at the dog, handling the dog roughly, and tying the lanyard too tight around the neck. These are just a few things observed. What must the dog endure out of sight of everyone? It's obvious the groomer's initial training was sadly lacking for these abuses to happen.

Many owners have requested the opportunity to watch the groomer groom their dog and have been politely, abruptly and sometimes rudely told "**NO you can't go into the grooming or bathing areas.**" "The dog will get excited and misbehave when the owner is there", is the excuse most often given by the groomer.

Why Not?

Why is the owner banned, really, from ensuring that their dog is treated properly, by observing the groomer in action?

There are many ways to have the excited dog behave and regain his focus and still allow the owner to watch the grooming session. (Chapter #9; Problems and Solutions):

Fact #1: the owner has the right to observe the groomer as they work on their dog. They are paying the groomer for a service and as such have the right to see what they are getting for their money. Groomer, you are being paid to perform a service on a **living animal** and unless you as the groomer have poor grooming practises to hide **allow the owner to observe the grooming session.**

Fact #2: the owners will also see how well their dog behaves and where extra basic training is required to improve the grooming session, plus the owner will see exactly how the groomer treats and handles their dog.

Fact #3: the groomer will get a better history of the dog by talking to the owner as they work. This relaxes the owner and in turn the dog picks up on the calmness of the owner and will relax too.

Fact #4: that word of mouth travels very fast whether the news is good or bad.

Owner, if you are happy with the service rendered on your dog and the dog is happy, leave a tip with your payment, spread the word and then go back to the groomer again. If you are not happy with the services, don't go back. If the dog receives injuries, the owner is not obligated to pay the bill, plus the owner is entitled to a truthful explanation of what happened, not vague excuses. If the injury is major and requires vet treatment, **remember,** the groomer is responsible for the injury occurring during the dog's stay at the salon. Above all the groomer/salon is to be made responsible for the vet bills pertaining to the injury.

Razor burns, nicks and chunks in the skin by the clippers, eyes poked by scissors. Tongues, feet and ears cut by scissors. Pieces of black blade guides imbedded in the skin which then become infected. Toe nails cut so short that it takes days for the bleeding to stop. Dogs hung and sustaining neck injuries. Dogs have died because they were left in drying kennels, with the heat on too high for too long. The list goes on.

There shouldn't be a list!

These injuries are a controlled form of negligence or animal abuse and the only way a **bad** groomer gets away with it, is basically implying you weren't there to witness what happened so you'll just have to take their word for it, as to what happened. **The dog's not going to talk.** Or the groomer doesn't say anything about the incident at all till the owner discovers the injury after they get the dog home. The groomer/salon's response to call back complaint is "That could have happened at any time after you left the salon". Once again the owner is left holding the bill, an injured dog and a whole lot of righteous anger.

Owners don't be afraid to give your dog a good once over **before** you pay the bill and leave the salon. Especially, when the dog's behaviour appears unusual. Owners you are not only your dogs' trusted companion, you are also their voice. Speak!

Groomer own up to the injury you caused to the dog. Tell the owner exactly what happened and if necessary offer to take care of the vet bills pertaining to the injuries, considering you are responsible for the injuries in the first place. At least knock the grooming price down if the injury is minor but still noticeable. Be careful next time you groom any animal.

Common sense and patience is required to be a decent groomer and believe me, there are some very good groomers out there.

Table Manners

Owner, your dog's table manners are an essential tool in the quality and time it takes to thoroughly complete your dog's grooming.

Sit and stay: the dog is required to sit on the table and not move.

Stand and stay: the dog is required to stand on the table and not move.

Hold: the dog is required to not move at all, the area that is being clipped or scissor, e.g. the face, especially around the eyes and mouth or the delicate skin areas like the groin and underarms.

No Teeth: This speaks for itself. No one likes to be bit or snapped at.

No Barking: Again very explicit, also for keeping the noise level under control.

Come: The dog needs to come to the groomer on command for picking up, following the groomer to the grooming table or bathing room.

Down: the dog is required to drop down on their belly, keep four feet on the floor or bend their head down or put their foot down.

Off: no jumping on people or furniture.

Lift: The dog is required to lift the foot you are holding for trimming of the nails, pad hair or washing/drying the foot and leg or to lift its head up.

Backup: The dog is required to back up in the tub and when the dog crowds the safety gate and doors.

Swing: Large dogs are required to turn around in the tub. The groomer turns the head towards themselves and into the direction they want the dog to face, then they say **swing** and the back end swings around to straighten the dog out. More often than not the groomer has to help the dog swing their bum around.

Groomer, politely inform the owner if the dog needs extra training in any of these areas. Let the owner know that it will be a big help during the grooming session. If the dog is well trained, praise him when he follows all of your directions. Thank the owner for their dog's beautiful table manners and the owner's training efforts with their dog. That it was a pleasure to groom such a well, behaved dog.

The Pickup Artist

A small dog is the easiest to pick up but the most unpredictable. Ask the dog to sit, when he does praise him. Approach the dog's side, bend your knees, slip your closet hand over the dog and place it under the chest just behind the under arms, spreading your fingers for maximum support. Lift the dog using that same arm to hold the dog snug to your hip. Use your elbow for back end support, like carrying a football. Take your free hand and place it over the neck and shoulders of the dog. Use your legs to lift yours and the dog's weight, into a standing position.

Leapers

To prevent the dog from leaping out of your arms, hook a finger into the collar to prevent a leaper from taking off.

Droppers

A dropper is a dog that is unsure or doesn't want to do what the you require of him. So he drops quickly to a flat, heavy, heap on the floor. This position makes it hard for you to pick them up and is a **passive aggressive** movement.

For the small dog, gently lift him into a sitting position by cupping your hand under the jaw bone and say **sit** when the dog is in the proper position. Praise the dog. Then lift the dog properly up into your arms and hook a finger into the collar for safety.

For larger dog, use a lanyard around their neck and say the dog's name and **come**. The dog gets up and will follow you. Praise the dog. As the dog is walking past the table or tub area, quickly slip your arm under the groin area preventing the dog's back end from dropping down, and then wrap your other arm across the front of the dog's chest, using your legs lift the dog up. If the dog is heavy or very large have two people, one at the front and one at the back end. Both of you are on the same side of the dog. The front person wraps one arm across the chest area and the other arm under the front legs. The back person wraps their arm under the lower belly and behind the bum for secure support. Both people lift at the same time, using their legs to lift properly and place the dog on the grooming table or in the tub.

Hoppers

A hopper is a small to medium size dog, that when picked up, will hop into your arms at the last second and crack you in the chin or mouth with their head. Ouch!

To prevent this painful connection, place your spread hand on the dogs shoulder blades and apply light continuous pressure. Wrap your other arm around and under the chest and snug that four legged football under your arm. The pressure on the shoulder blades will **check** the sudden last second hop before it starts. You will feel the **check** work as the dog tries to hop.

Hiders

A hider is a small dog that will slink away and run around the table, their owner, or hide under something to get away from you. This is another passive aggressive move the dog does to achieve what it wants. To prevent this frustrating game, say the dog's name, then, direct it to **sit and stay**. You'll know quickly if the dog has been trained well because it will automatically sit for you. Praise the dog. Then gently pick the dog up, properly.

When the dog hides behind the owner, get the owner to step back and away from the dog, preferably against a wall to prevent the hiding. Direct the dog into a **sit and stay,** then, lift the dog up properly. If the dog doesn't sit when directed, politely ask the owner to work some more on the **sit and stay** training with their dog at home.

Triangles and Pears

Triangles and Pears refer to the body shape on certain breeds of dog and the overweight dog. Dogs that have a broad, deep chest, that have a small compact back end, are triangular in shape. They are very top heavy. Bulldogs are a fine example of a triangular shape dog. I had the pleasure of knowing a bulldog named Harley, to practise the proper lift with. I finally found one that worked the best for us, both; because he is a solid weight and an awkward shape to lift safely.

Have the dog jump on a low couch, slip one arm under the groin area, hand up and flat towards the spine. Take your other arm and slide it **between** the front legs and hold just behind the shoulder.

Take a deep breath, keep your spine straight and lift using your legs and blow the air out as you lift. The dog is balanced in your arms with this type of lift and using your legs is a must to prevent back stain or groin muscle pull.

Pear shaped dogs are small and narrow at the shoulders and upper chest and become rounder and heavier in the belly and bum area. Slip your arm **around** the bum area and your other arm under the front legs, hand up and over the shoulder. Lift using your legs and cradle the dog in a sitting position against your chest.

All these lifts keep the dog balanced and secure in your arms. Always use your legs to lift to prevent back and groin strains. Not all dogs know how or want to climb a ramp, jump up on the table or into the bathtub. More often than not it is faster, safer and easier to lift, or help lift a dog where you need it to be.

Large Dogs and the Table or Tub

For a large dog, let him do most of the work. Encourage the dog by pointing on to the **lowered** table or into the tub and say their name and the direction, **Cookie, up.** Most large dogs will jump onto the table or into the tub, no problem. Praise them. If they only get their front feet up but not their back end, due to age, hip or back problems, praise them and say firmly **stay.** Bend your knees and slide one arm under the lower belly in front of the hind legs and your other arm supporting the bum under the tail. Lift with your legs. When the dog is on the table or in the tub, praise them again.

Table Turns

There are a few quick, easy ways to turn a dog around or into the position you require for grooming. Make a V with your fingers and thumb on each hand. Place one hand under and along the dog's jaw bone and the other in front of the hind legs, under the belly/groin area. Lift the dog up and turn it around to the direction you require. For ¼ turns lift by the jaw bone or belly/groin area to reposition the dog. If the dog is bigger or belly heavy use your arm by sliding it under the belly/groin area and lifting the back end into position on the table.

When turning an extra small or light weight dog, place your hand under the rib cage and lift and turn the dog into place. Always turn the dog smoothly and gently, they won't struggle when they are in mid turn. If you have a nervous dog on your table that panics every time you lift and turn them, say **turn** then lift and turn the dog into position. I have two poodle crosses that use to hang on to me with all four legs, every time I lifted them to turn them on the table. I started pre-warning them with **turn** then I would lift and turn them. They knew what was coming and remained calm. They were praised every time.

How to Properly Handle the Tools of Your Trade

Scissors:

The minimum number of scissors required is 3 pair. One 6.5 inch curved shears, one 5 inch hair dressing scissors, rounded tips and one pair of thinning shears with 30 teeth. With an increase in your clientele, backup pairs of scissors are needed to replace the first pairs when they become dull and need to be sent out for sharpening.

Scissors are a personal preference in regards to style, colour, length, weight and balance. Balance in your choice of scissors is very important. Test the balance by working the scissors in your hand. Some pairs feel better in your hand then others.

Finger placement for comfort and quick release to prevent accidents is crucial for maximum control of your scissors. The thumb and **ring finger** sit in the finger holes. The scissor holes **do not** go past the first knuckle bone on these fingers. When purchasing your scissors your finger hole measurement should be only to the first knuckle, no further. This is your **quick release** safety guide. So be selective and test how quickly you are able to take your thumb out of the handle loop. Is it too loose, to snug or just right?

To properly hold your scissors, first, your baby finger **rests** on the finger rest, your ring finger rests **in** the finger loop above the finger rest **only to the first knuckle**. Your tall man rests above the ring finger loop and your pointer rests above your tall man. Your thumb is in the top finger loop **half way to the first knuckle.**

If you are not cutting with the scissors, take your thumb out of the finger loop and fold all four of your fingers, still in position on your scissors, into your palm. This keeps the blades **closed** and the scissors at the ready in a **safe** position in your hand till you need them. When you do need to use them, unfold your fingers flat, the scissors will automatically roll with your fingers into position for the thumb to quickly slip smoothly into its finger loop.

This is a move that you need to practice because it will be used often while working on a dog or cat. These animals move quickly and you don't need to be fumbling with your equipment and fingers. You need to be quicker and smoother than your client.

Scissor positions most used are 6, 9, and 12 o'clock. If you are left handed your positions are 6, 3 and 12 o'clock. Any scissor positions past these numbers and you lose **safety control** of your scissors around a moving animal and the client **will** get hurt.

5" inch scissors are for trimming between the pads, straight lines and around the eyes and trimming ears. Curved 6.5" scissors are a dream for a smooth curve on paws, to follow the curve of the body, head, ears or legs. Curved scissors are reversible and have a finger rest on each finger loop, so you don't lose control of your scissors in the convex or concave position.

The finger positions are exactly the same in concave/convex position. You just have to practice turning the scissors in your hand quickly and smoothly.

Hold the scissors in your hand, fingers in the proper positions. Remove your thumb from the finger loop and place it just above the finger loop to hold the scissors steady. Then, remove your ring finger from its loop and roll the scissors towards your thumb with your 4 fingers till the scissors have turned over. Insert your ring finger in the new loop and place all fingers in their positions then insert your thumb into its new loop and you are now ready to trim on the opposite curve. Start slowly till your fingers become familiar with the movement then increase your speed till you are fast and smooth.

Always remember, your client moves fast on the table, you have to be faster, smoother and safer.

Thinning Shears are for thinning out the hair. You hold the thinning shears the same as regular scissors but when it comes to cutting, the technique is totally different.

To thin eyebrows which require light thinning, you cut half way up from the root section and then close to the top of the hair shaft. Take two snips at a time till you get the right texture and look you are trying to achieve. Always cut in increments with the thinning shears and never in the same spot or too close to the roots. Feathers and pants can be thinned out using the **<** or **>** technique. This technique removes bulk but keeps the shape and length of the feathers and pants. Start at the bottom of the feather or pant leg and work your way up in half inch thick, horizontal sections. Comb the hair section straight out from the leg and cut a **<** or **>** shape in the center of the section between the roots and the ends. Comb the cut/thinned hair out of the section. Caution, not all feathers or pants, need to be thinned out. A good thorough brushing will usually do the trick but now and then you will come across a thick set of feathers or pants that will need to be thinned. Thin carefully because you don't want these sections to look too thin when you are done. If it means thinning every second section or only the thickest part of the feathers or pants then use your common sense and apply the thinning shears accordingly.

When trimming the tail, don't leave it looking unnaturally blunt, take your thinning shears and thin the blunt edge a 1/2 to an inch from the ends. Thinning the blunt ends will give the trimmed tail a softer more natural finish.

Always keep your scissors sharp and the tips rounded not pointed. Clean the blades in Barbicide and use a drop of clipper oil on the screw to lubricate.

When your scissors are at rest on the grooming table make sure they are **closed.** Remember, your client is always moving on your grooming table. Open, sharp scissor blades and moving, soft paws are an accident waiting to happen.

Clippers

There are a lot of different brands and styles of clippers out on the market. The proper, professional clipper to use in a grooming salon is the clipper that has different stainless steel blade heads that snap on and locked into place on the clipper body by a blade lock. Toss the plastic, clip on blade guides in the trash!

The clipper blades are stainless steel and are easily cleaned with a tooth brush to remove hair and then oiled and can be cleaned and sanitized in Barbicide or a sterilizer. The blades range in size according to numbers and are interchangeable on most brands of clipper bodies. The blades have three parts, the bottom blade, the top blade and a plastic glide that reduces friction as the top blade is moved back and forth by the toggle on the clippers.

A round shape clipper body is recommended so that you can easily roll it in your hand to change the angle of the blade while you are clipping. The clippers need to have a blade lock on it so your blade doesn't pop off when you clip through a dense section of hair on your client.

You will need a **minimum** of 2 pairs of the same type of clippers, on hand at all times. The second pair is a backup for when your first clippers break down or need regular maintenance. Clean and always check the condition of your clippers **daily.** Change the blade toggle when it wears or your blades will not perform properly.

Keep the electrical cord to the outside of the hand that holds the clippers. This will keep the cord from tangling around the table and prevent you from stepping on the cord as well. If you need to put the clippers down on the grooming table, place the clippers on the end of the table, blade in, electric cord hanging over the end. This prevents you from tripping over the cord or your client from knocking the clippers off the table. Or install a large cup hook to the underside of your table and hook your clippers safely out of the way of moving paws.

To properly handle your clippers, hold the clipper body in your hand like a pen with the back of the clippers resting in the arch of the thumb and pointer. The electric cord arcs over the back of your hand and is aimed parallel to the back of your arm. This position gives you the most control over the clippers. It keeps the cord out of your visual work area and allows you to quickly turn the clippers around without losing control of them during grooming. Practice turning your clippers, so the blade is in the different positions you will use in order to groom your client.

Always test the temperature of the blade on the inside of your forearm, if the blade is hot change it for a cool one. Change the blades often as they heat up from friction and will be **very** uncomfortable for the client. Let the hot blade cool down on your table out of the way. Also, make sure you have the proper blade number locked on the clippers before you resume clipping.

Maintain your clippers by using a tooth brush and clean the hair, thoroughly, from the area where the blade sits, plus any nooks and crannies where hair can collect. If your clippers are air cooled, clean the air intake screen also. Oil or grease your clippers according to manufacturer's specifications. Have the clippers maintained on a regular basis, replacing the toggle and or brushes when they become worn.

Cleaning your clipper blades is the most important section, **because if your blades don't work, neither do you**. First and foremost, keep your blades sharp. Keep your blades oiled and hair free **every day**. Clean your blades in Barbicide or a sterilizer after each client.

Brush all the hair off the entire surface of the blade including between the tines. To clean the hair out from between the blade plates, push the top plate sideways with a toothbrush till it is ½ way past the bottom plate, use your baby finger to stop the top plate from sliding all the way out. Brush all the hair off from both plates then slide the top blade to the other end of the bottom plate till its ½ way out again and clean the other side of both plates. Before you close the top plate back into place, put a drop of oil on the bars located on the bottoms of both plates. Keep your blades in numerical order and lay them on a towel to absorb excess oil. Have your clippers and your blades within reach of the grooming table.

The minimum number of each blade you use most, to keep you working is ten (10). When your blade gets dull, set it aside in a container and take out a sharp one. The dull blades are to be taken to your blade sharpening person, someone who has taken a special, specific course in clipper blade sharpening. Dull blades will not cut the hair properly, will bind in the hair, will create corduroy hair, will chunk the hair, as well as pull the hair as it cuts. Most of all, dull blades will cause **razor burn**. **Keep your blades sharp.**

Nail Trimmers

Having tried all types of nail trimmer, the pair that gives the best visibility of the nail, the quick and cutting area is the scissor style trimmers. When purchasing this style of trimmer, line up a few different makes on their sides and choose the thinner of the stainless steel heads. It will give you maximum view of the quick and cutting areas. Purchase a minimum of 6 pairs per year depending on the volume of nails you trim annually. Clean them with Barbicide or sterilizer. Maintain with a drop of oil on the screw head. If you cut a client's quick and it bleeds, make sure your clean the trimmer blades thoroughly before using them on your next client, because a dog's nose is a heck of a lot more sensitive than ours and to have a bloody piece of equipment come at you, that is known to cause pain if improperly used, will have your client baulking even more, at having their nails trimmed.

Some groomers prefer the dremmel tool to file the nails down instead of cutting. These are fine but be very careful. They create friction and will heat the nail up very fast if you are not careful. Just the same way they do in a nail salon for humans.

Brushes

A slicker brush is a must in the grooming salon. You will need a minimum of two at all times. One slicker each, for the grooming and drying tables. You will go through three to seven slickers annually depending on the amount of clients you have. Always keep an eye on the condition of the tines. If you've lost more than 2 tines toss the brush because the tines start breaking off faster and you lose the brush's full potential.

A natural boar's bristle brush is another good brush for the salon. The boars bristle brush does not scratch the skin on short haired clients. This type of brush takes the natural oils in the hair and distributes it evenly throughout the hair shaft, roots to ends, leaving the hair shiny and healthy looking. Better penetration, to the skin can be achieved by more space between bristles. The bristles need to be very stiff. The bristle stiffness test is running your thumb through the different boars bristle brushes for sale. Next the bristles must be set into a solid wood or plastic brush body. They will last 3 to 4 times longer than the bristles that are set in a rubber cushion, which is then set into a brush body. The bristles can get pushed into the rubber cushion making the bristles uneven, therefore extremely less efficient and a waste of your hard earned money.

Any other brushes would be a personal choice. Find the brushes that suit and work best for you and your clients. Then buy them in multiples.

Combs

Combs are again, a personal choice, steel, wood, plastic, colour, number of teeth, style, length etc. etc. etc. The important thing to remember is that the body and the teeth of the comb need to be solid in construction with no seams or burrs that can snag, pull stretch or break the hair shaft. The teeth for everyday use should be 1/16th of an inch apart. Plus the body of the comb should not bend in your hand during use.

A pick comb with 12 steel tines, set 1/3 of an inch apart is an excellent tool to use with your clippers to achieve a longer length hair cut. Picks are not proper combs, they are used to lift the hair up and out for volume. Lift the hair to the desired length and then use the clippers to clip off the excess hair on the outside of the tines.

Combs that look like a sturdy garden rake in miniature are call rakes. A 4 inch wide head with 30 stainless steel tines an 1/8th of an inch apart and 1 inch long tines is a good all round tool for all hair types. Make sure this comb is solid construction from top to bottom because if the head is just set in the handle it will eventually be pulled out from constant use. The rake is used to remove large volumes of hair and under coat. You must do a preliminary brush through with the slicker brush first, then, use the rake in long even strokes through the hair to remove the excess. You can also line rake the hair especially where the hair is thicker.

Barbicide

Barbicide is a commercial bactericide, fungicide and virucide. Hair salons have been using this product for decades to clean combs, scissors, blades, brushes etc. This product is a very important tool in the grooming salon.

Here are just a few potential, but very real examples of what your blades, scissors, brushes and combs go through on just about every client that stands on your grooming table. Dust, dander mud, bacteria, sweat, bacteria, drool, bacteria, tears and tear crustiness, bacteria, nose mucus, bacteria, stuck on food, bacteria, oily hair, straw, grass, sap, pine needles, old scabs, bacteria, fresh wounds, bacteria, blood, bacteria, cauliflower and weeping warts, bacteria and viruses, sebaceous cysts, bacteria, fleas, lice, ticks, maggots, urine, stool and bacteria. Did I miss anything? Oh yeah...**BACTERIA.**

Sterilizers

The ultimate cleaning weapon for any salon is the sterilizer. There are many different brands of Autoclave sterilizers and UV sterilizers. They will sterilize all the equipment that touches your clients. That includes blades, combs, brushes, scissors etc. Add this equipment to your must have list and it will pay for itself in appreciative owners because you have ensured the health and safety of their beloved pet.

Lanyards

I have renamed the neck noose to lanyard because of the negative connotations the word noose implies and considering all the dogs that have had the unpleasant and life threatening experience of being hung, I'd like to think positively and apply a **safety first** to this very important paragraph.

NEVER USE ONE LANYARD ON SMALL TO MEDIUM SIZE CLIENTS

Two lanyards clipped on the loop of a swivel clip which is then clipped to the loop on the grooming arm. One lanyard loop goes around the neck and under opposite underarm. The second lanyard loops around the lower belly just in front of the hind legs. Now you can lower the pinch clips loosely for safety.

The double lanyard comes in very handy on clients that tend to sit when you work on their back end and tail, for the older client with back and hip problems, for young active clients that tend to dance all over the grooming table, skittish clients and for the clients that twist around into pretzels to avoid or interfere with your grooming.

A word of caution in the lanyard placement on a male client, ensure that the penis is cradled in the lanyard loop for comfort and is not bent. Also, some of your clients will have a heavier/wider back end and will need to have the height of the back lanyard lower for comfort.

Two lanyards and a collar is another safety method of securing clients on the table that twist and turn so much that you can't see the area you need to work on, more often than not it's the feet and nails. Secure the client in the double lanyard method then using their collar, loop the collar around the back lanyard strap and clip it around the grooming arm. This will stop the hind end movement totally. The client is secure, and now very safe for you to start cutting nails or trimming feet and pads. When the client ceases to twist, praise them, keeping your voice low and even. Dogs are smart, when they realize you are not hurting them their table manners will greatly improve.

Grooming Arm

The grooming arm is attached to the grooming table by a special clamp. The arm is a **7** shape and is adjustable in height. At the top of the arm is a loop where the lanyard clips are attached. Always check that the clamp and height adjustable screws are tight to prevent the arm from falling down or the entire unit from falling off the table.

Grooming Table

When purchasing your grooming table, a good size table top is 42 inches long and 24 inches wide. This size will accommodate all client sizes except large to extra-large size dogs which should be groomed on the floor any ways.

An electric grooming table is the best, there are hydraulic and stationary tables available but are not as smooth raising or lowering or as easy on your back as the electric. The electric table can be lowered from to 19 inches to a height of 41 inches from the floor, for any size client and for comfort to your back. Clean the table top, arm and table foot print and jack on a regular basis with Barbicide.

Shampoos and Conditioners

In any salon, human or canine, how well you've cleaned the hair will make or break the overall style. After 39 years working with **all kinds** of hair you get to know and use hundreds of different kinds of shampoos and conditioners.

The best shampoo to use is one that cleans all hair types thoroughly, have little or no perfume, a low surfactant (suds), easily and quickly rinses out of the hair, is lower on the **ph.** scale and leaves hair squeaky clean after **one** shampoo. The same thing is required for dog shampoo. The big difference is human skin leans towards the acidic side of the ph. scale while dog skin leans towards the alkali side of the ph. scale. The skin ph. is different, hence the difference in dog and human shampoos. So, if you've been using your perfumed acidic human shampoo on your dog, **STOP!**

The conditioner needs to be light weight in texture, non-sticky or waxy, good penetration into the hair shaft, rinses quickly and helps rinse any lingering, shampoo residue, dander, loose hair and is good for **all hair types.** Shampoos clean dirt and oils etc. from the **skin and hair**, while conditioners penetrate and coat the hair shaft, they condition not clean. The good news, you can use a good quality human conditioner for coloured hair on your dog' hair.

How do I know this? Because I've tried the market dog conditioners and I ended up tossing them in the trash along with the hair balls. I went to my trusty salon supplier and got samples of conditioners for normal hair, plus the tubes of conditioner I had from my hair colour box, to try out in my grooming salon. The coloured hair conditioner won hands down because some of the conditioners were too heavy for fine candy floss hair on Maltese, for example and too light for light, course dry hair on for example, a Sheltie. The coloured hair conditioner is light weight, penetrated into the hair shaft quickly and thoroughly, I only needed a little to condition the dog's hair and best of all it worked on all the different dog hair types with fantastic results. The course hair on the Shelties and Rough Collies remained course in texture but didn't tangle or feel dry to the touch. The candy floss fine hair of Maltese or Chinese Crested Powder Puff, silky hair of Yorkshire Terriers, combo hair on Shih Tzu crosses were unbelievable soft and tangle free and the hair flowed when the dog moved.

Drying time was very quick, the long hair didn't tangle nearly as much and brushed out very quickly. The loose hair slid off the dog during drying and the hair was soft and manageable without losing the feel of the different textures.

I called the L'Oréal Company in Montreal, to find out what conditioner in the professional market was equivalent to their boxed hair colour conditioner and could I get it in bulk? I was told L'Oréal Expert Vitamin O for coloured hair. It is the only conditioner I use in my salon. One operator at the L'Oréal Company wasn't impressed that I wanted to use their product on dogs and told me not to mention it when I spoke to any other operators. But the basic part of L'Oréal's business is **hair** and to **sell hair products.** If their product can be used in another, lucrative hair avenue, what's the problem? It's all hair and it's all profit coming in from sales and that's the bottom line in business. Plus the product is good or I wouldn't use it exclusively in my salon.

Bath Tubs

There are many different tubs available for the grooming salon. Stainless steel is the best because it doesn't chip if you drop something heavy in it or scratch from the client's nails. Stainless steel cleans easily and with a couple of rubber bath mats on the bottom of the tub the client will have a better footing.

Use a good professional, steel hosed, shower head with a shut off toggle in the handle to save water and you won't have to keep adjusting the water temperature during the bath. When you've finished bathing the client turn the taps off. In the drain place a stainless steel, fitted strainer to catch the hair and allow the water to drain free. You can find these in any kitchen and bath store. Have a small wire strainer hooked to the top of your tub to put the balls of hair removed from the drain strainer into. This will allow the hair balls to drip dry and then be thrown into the garbage, preventing mould.

Keep your shampoo and conditioner bottles confined and outside of the tub. The only thing that should be in the tub beside your client is the shower head, mats and water. Have a side table next to the tub to hold shampooing items, as well as towels. Finally you'll need two lanyards to secure your client in the tub so they don't jump out.

Dryers

There are again, many different types and styles of dryers. The top four **safe** dryers are large cotton and shamwow style towels, electric stand dryers with four heat settings, 4 and 8 horsepower blaster dryers using ambient air, reducing your drying time substantially and in the spring and summer natural warm air and sunshine. **From experience, it is a lot faster to dry your clients with the above mentioned drying units.**

Kennel dryers should be your last choice of dryer if at all, because most clients are excessively stressed by kennel dryers and most of all, because dogs have died in kennel dryers. **It is safer to leave this expensive liability off your purchase list.**

Garbage Cans

Garbage cans are essential to keep the mess contained in you salon. You'll need one 121 liter plastic garbage can with a lid. This size of can takes the orange or clear yard/leaf plastic bags. Put a vanillaroma tree in the bottom of the can, it's the only scented tree that will make an outhouse smell good. Believe me I've tried them all and vanillaroma is the best.

You will need smaller cans with plastic bags at all the work stations, grooming and drying tables, desk, lunch room, bathroom, tub area, laundry room and one with a lid, outside for stool only. Never throw stool into an inside garbage can because there is nothing worse that the smell of stool every time you open the garbage can lid. So, help keep your salon smelling clean by storing the stool outside in a plastic bag lined garbage can with a lid.

Essential Oils

Lavender oil is used to help calm the nervous client by putting a drop on each corner of the towel that covers the grooming and drying tables, or on the soft cloth muzzle for clients that bite, to help calm them too.

Aloe Vera gel is used to clean eyes and ears and to soften the crusties under the eyes.

Citronella oil is used to help control fleas, tick and lice that get carried in the salon by your clients and also to help loosen the chunks created by ear mites in your client's ears.

Mirrors

The most valuable piece of equipment needed and most used in your salon is a couple of full length mirrors. Not for you silly, for your clients. Place the mirror on the floor and attached to the wall to reflect the entire grooming table. This positioning gives you full reflection of the client on the grooming table. You can see how your work is progressing, if you miss a spot etc.

The second advantage to having mirrors is that the client watches what you are doing to them. I have had clients face the mirror and refuse to move, so I had to move around the grooming table to work on them. The client was very cooperative as long as they stayed facing the mirror so they could watch.

I had a little Maltese on my table that was very nervous, so I introduced the clippers to her and made a small pass of the blade on her fur. She had already discovered the mirror and was watching the clippers clip her hair. She watched the hair fall to the table then she turned her body towards the mirror to see the results and she wagged her tail. After that she checked the hair cut progress herself, in the mirror till the end. I was fascinated watching her watch me, working on her.

Thirdly, mirrors are used by the owners to watch how you work on their dogs. Nothing is hidden from them and they can view the progress from different angles. I have had many pleased comments on the mirror positioning and the fact that I have such large mirrors for the dogs to admire themselves, before during and after grooming.

Dogs, as clients are very self-aware and love to look at themselves in the mirror, so don't be stingy with these majorly important and highly entertaining pieces of equipment.

Kennels in the Salon

Ok so, how many of you work in a salon that keeps the clients kennelled? Do you go home every night with your ears ringing from all the barking and whining? Raise your hands.

The reason the clients do this is because they are not kennelled at home and more often than not the client has to **go.** Most Clients have the run of their house and back yards. The client is stressed because they were kennelled and were vocal about it, which in turn stresses you out which in turn stresses the client out more because they picked up on your stress. Worst of all after you've clipped washed dried fluffed and put a bandana on the client, you put them in the kennel and the client does their business in the kennel because there is nowhere else to go unless they escape and do a quick squat and release before you can catch them. There's another mess to clean up, eh? Not to mention the mess on your nice clean client from walking through the kennel mess. Grrr!

Another way, a better way to have a quiet stress free, salon is to play a wide variety of music that is pleasing to the ear, windows for the clients to see what's going on outside. Pillows, chairs, couches fresh water bowels, and a fenced in yard with a dog door access for your clients to independently go when needed. Best of all there are no kennels and no continuous barking or whining and messes are kept to an extreme minimum. The clients come in, check out the rooms and greet any other clients already there. The client learns to socialize, relax and enjoy their time at the salon. This produces better salon behaviour and the clients are pleased to return. The clients are happy, you are happy and the owner is happy that their dog is happy.

High Five!!

Scissors

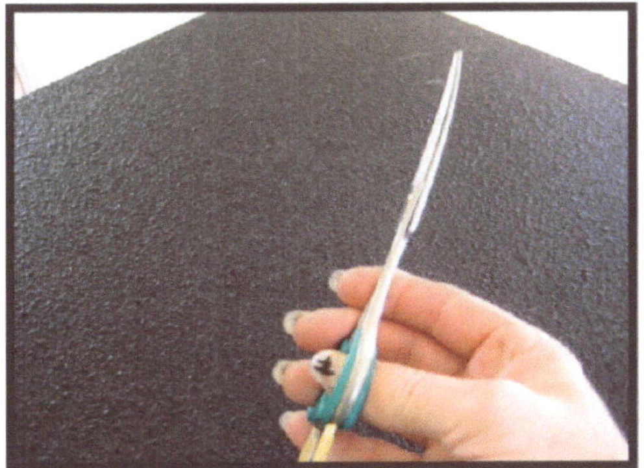

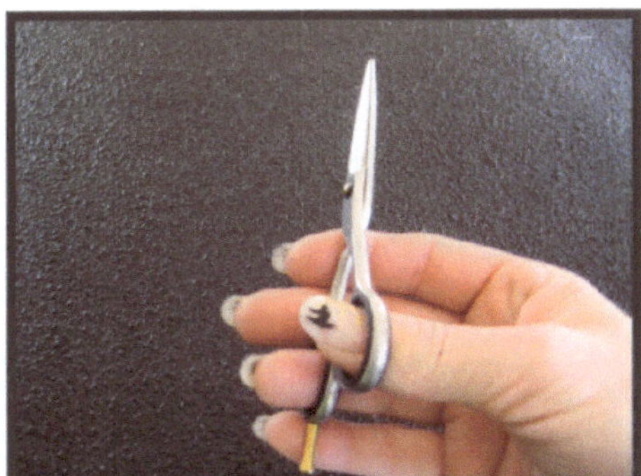

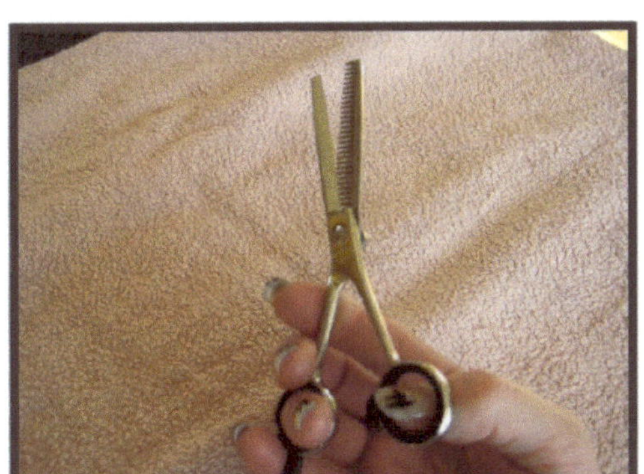

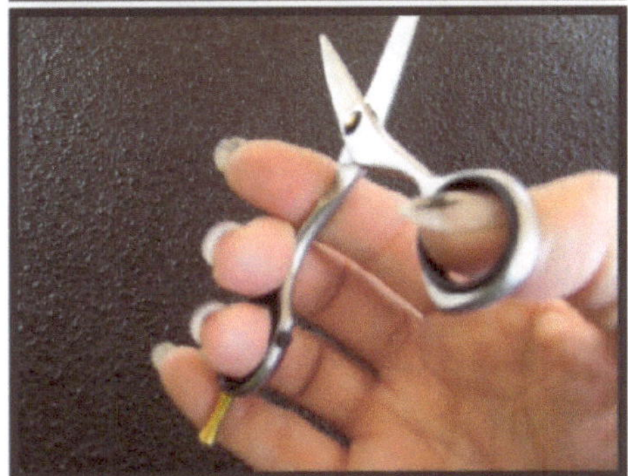

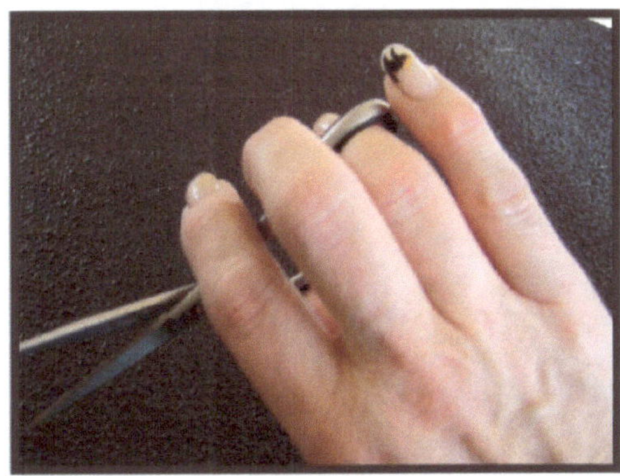

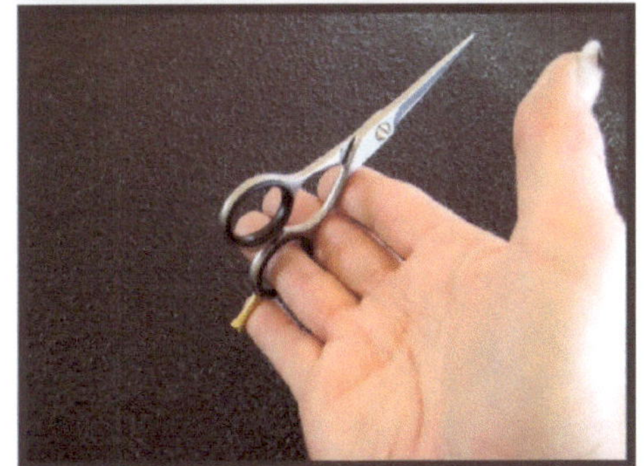

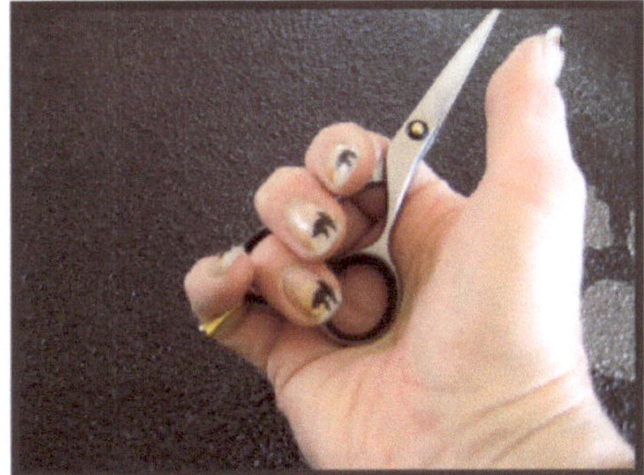

That Extra Scratch Behind the Ear Renaissance grooming

Clippers & Blades

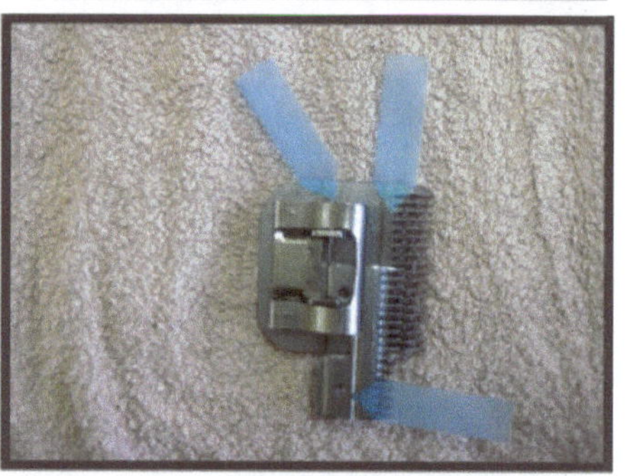

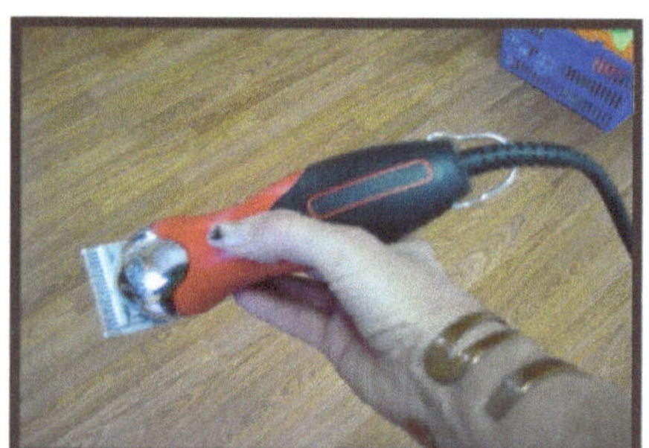

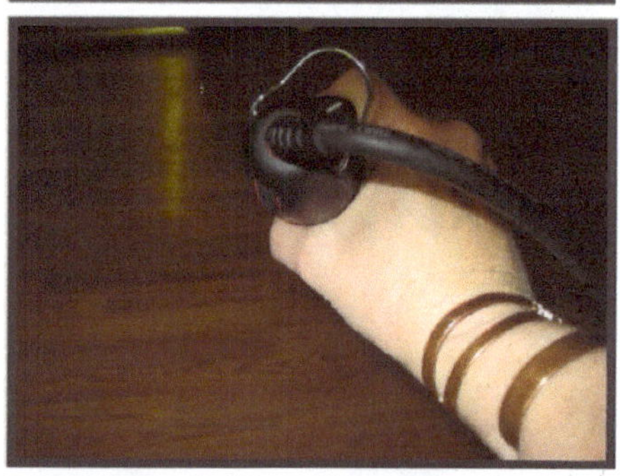

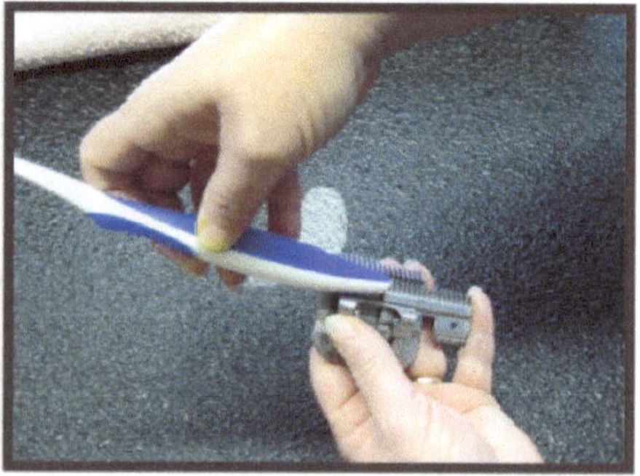

Nail Trimmers

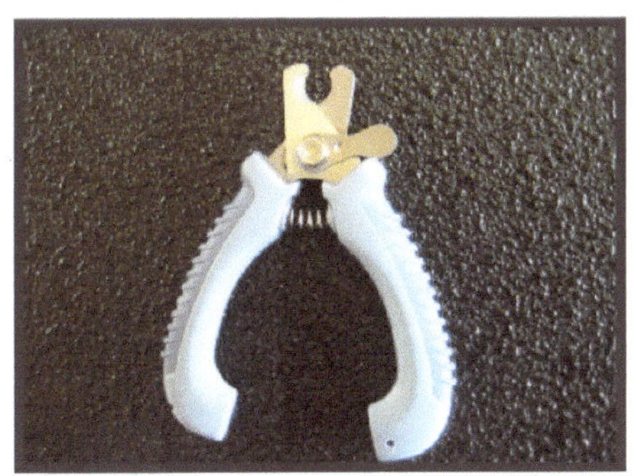

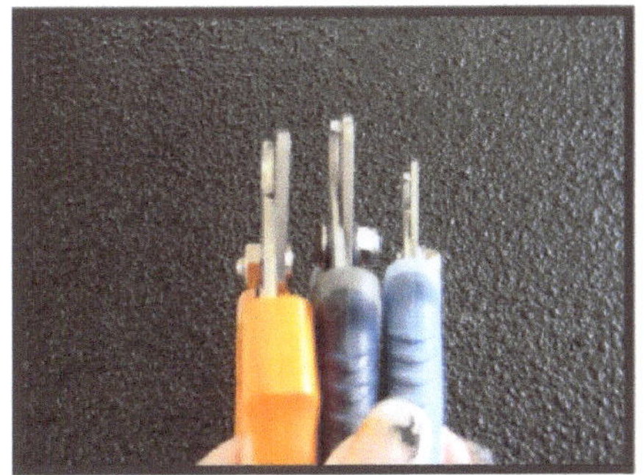

Brushes and Combs

Lanyards

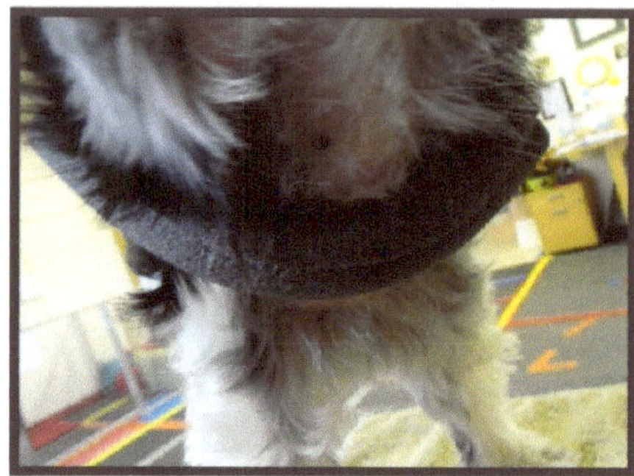

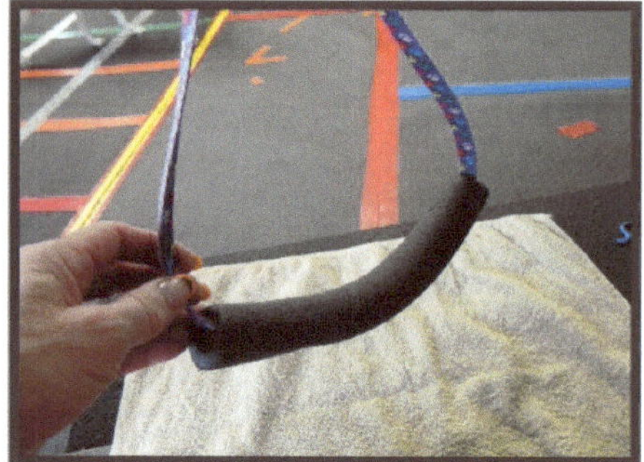

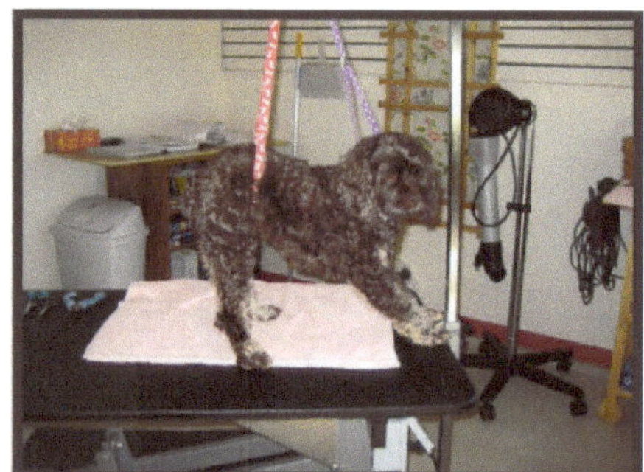

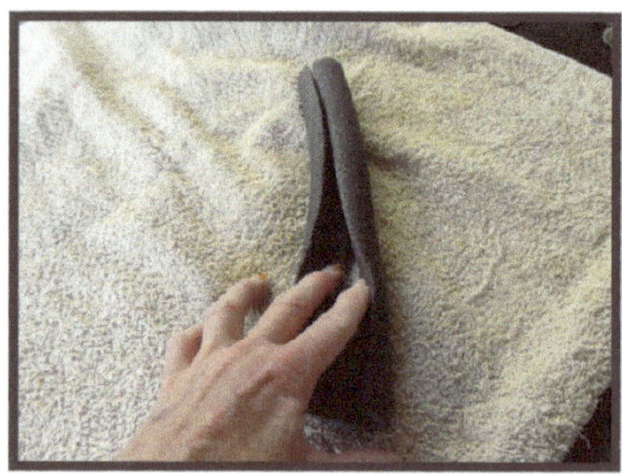

Daycare Fun

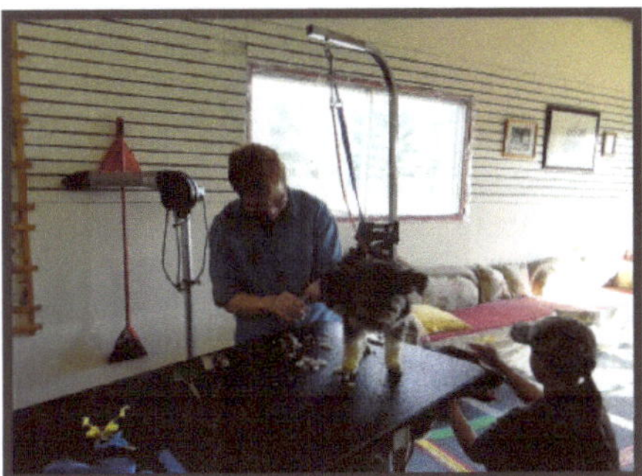

Mirrors

Dryers

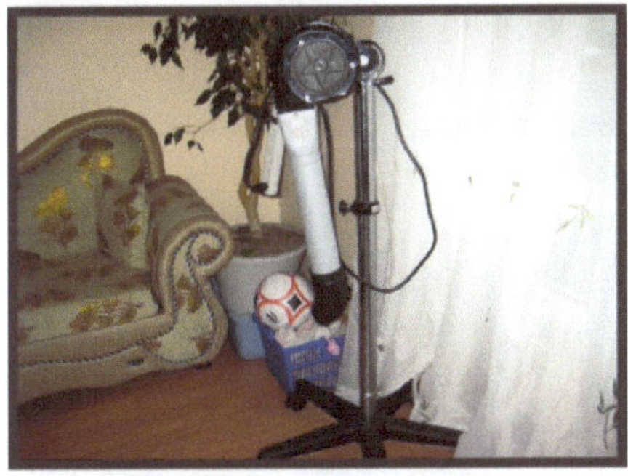

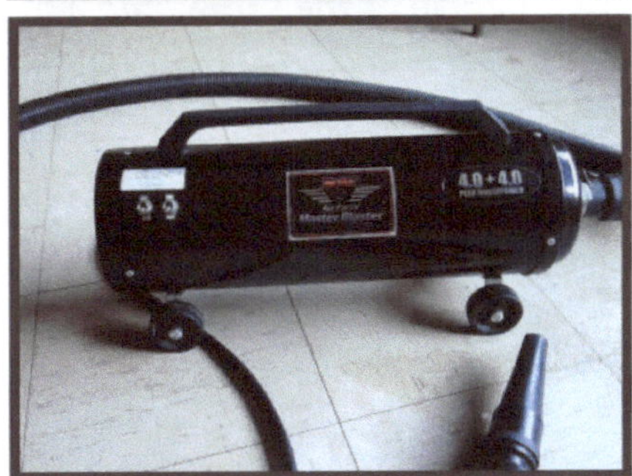

Proper Grooming Techniques for Owners and Groomers

When I first started grooming, I of course started in a pet store chain. As a hairstylist for humans, I found out real fast, that the pet store chain was the best place to find out how the worst of all grooming habits started, because the store is all about money and how much you, as a groomer can bring in as profit. The dogs are secondary. Their comfort and your comfort really don't count. There is no room for the dogs to play and socialize and definitely no place for the dog to go to the bathroom or even a bowl of fresh water to drink! This produced a very high stress location for both dog and groomer. No wonder the dog baulks at going through the door.

The production line was, in my estimation, **the worst** way to groom any dog. All of the dogs booked for the day were dropped off first thing in the morning and picked up at the end of the day. All that barking, yapping, whining, kennel cleaning, music that is jarring, three or more groomers jammed into a small area using poor to mediocre grooming tables and equipment...**Stop the bus I want off!!**

How can any groomer meet the individual needs of each different dog personality, if you use the production line method of grooming? Would you like your hairstylist to divide his or her time and talents between 6 or 7 people **at the same time** and try to keep the conversation straight as well as the individual hair needs? Not in this universe or the next!

So why do it to the dogs?!! I started planning a better method and a better salon setup for dogs after my first day.

On the average it takes 1 ½ hours to do a full groom on a small to medium size dog. Less time for just a bath and brush or body tidy (nails included). For double coated or matted dogs it will take approximately 2 hours to groom. So, with that in mind book your day accordingly every hour and a half.

You can book three to six dogs a day depending on size and time needed to do these dogs. If they are regular clients you'll know exactly how long it takes to groom them through your client grooming records. The only time the dogs arrive in multiples is if the owner has two or more dogs and you book them back to back.

Remember, one dog at a time. Your time is allotted to that one dog from start to finish and that client should have your full attention.

So, this is the part of the book where everything you learned in your particular grooming course, but the basics, toss out the window because this is how it's should be done, properly on your client.

Groomers, you will learn the faster more efficient way to groom your client. It will cut down on your grooming time and you become use to an easy routine without losing track of where you left off if interrupted. You will get into a rhythm and relax because it is used on all breeds of dog. No **production line**, one client at a time from start to finish.

Owners that want to groom their dogs themselves, here is your chance to learn as well.

The first rule of thumb for anyone who grooms a dog: **Never, ever hit or abuse your client!**

Keeping this foremost in your mind, lift the client properly onto the table. Loop the lanyards around the client's neck and lower belly. Remove the client's collar and allow them to smell it. Almost all will thoroughly smell the collar from end to end, or lick or nudge the collar and wag their tail. The client is acknowledging his own scent. This indicates that they will be cooperative on the table. The client that just sniffs once or turns its head away from the collar scent has had problems on another grooming table in the past and will likely give you grief because of it.

This is your first indication as to the client's attitude so pay close attention. Attach the collar to the grooming arm so you don't lose it.

This is the routine I established for all of my clients. It's quick, easy to remember and you don't lose track of where you left off if interrupted. So, let's jump in and start with the feet first.

Nails and Feet

The nails are the worst part of grooming for both client and groomer so you get the worst over with first, then, the rest of the grooming session will be relatively stress free and easy in comparison.

Have the client face you on the table. Hold the right front paw in your hand, between your pointer and tall man fingers. Using your thumb, push the hair up and away from the nail. Start with the dew claw and then the inside nail working your way to the outside nail. Then do the same with the left front paw and then the back left paw and finally the back right paw. Always check each paw for dew claws, some sit higher that others and some hide in the hair. The dew claw in some cross-breed or poorly bred dogs, have been found almost beside the other nails or **behind** the foot, not on the side.

The next step is to trim the hair around the feet. Once again start with the right front paw. Using the trimmed nails as your guideline and using the curved scissors, trim the outline of the paw. Then brush the hair up between each toe and trim hair the length needed to be blended in with the rest of the leg hair. Hold the paw gently but firmly. If the client pulls its paw back, say **No** firmly, when the client complies praise them. If the client continues to pull back hold the leg at the elbow to prevent the pull back. Praise the client when you are done.

Next turn the client to face away from you and lift the front right paw so the pad is up, trim the hair between the pads. Slide your finger between the large and small pads and pull the hair to the outside of the paw and trim. Slide your fingers between the toes from the top of the toes to the pads to get any long hair that was missed. Trim hair level with the pads.

When the right front paw is finished do the left front paw, then the left hind paw then the right hind paw. Praise the dog for co-operating with each section as your groomed. Always position the client so you have maximum access to each paw. Keep to the routine as this will help with accuracy and then speed. Learn to **be accurate first**, then, pick up your speed. Speed before accuracy causes injuries, not only to the dog but to you as well.

Another reason to stick to the routine is because the client becomes familiar with it as well and some will anticipate the next move by lifting the next paw or turning into the next position. This is fabulous because **trust** has been established as well as the routine and the **beginnings of good communication and co-operation**. The client remembers the routine and is comfortable with it and you. Don't forget to praise them when they anticipate.

The Face, Head, Muzzle and Eyes

The face is the next important section to groom because the client needs to see. All dogs have a dew lap under their chin. This is a loose flap of skin with no vital veins, muscles etc. Firmly grasp the dew lap between the thumb and bent pointer. This will control the head without hurting the client. Please note that some clients will simply lay their muzzle in your palm and not move, while some clients will jerk their heads out of your grasp at the last second or continuously. Some breeds are notorious for this but, as in everything, you have your good and your bad and you just learn to work around it without force or pain to your client.

So, holding the face in place by the dew lap or muzzle, use a **clean** #10 blade and clippers or small scissors and trim the hair away from the eyes. Using clippers trim the hair on top of the head and down the sides of the face to desired length, using caution around the eyes. Lift the ear up and trim the excess from under the base of the ear. This is the start of the balanced look on the head. (No bobble heads please)

Carefully clip the hair from under the eyes. This removes excess hair that causes eyes to tear and trap crusties that smell and hold bacteria. Remember these are family pets not show dogs, they need to see where they are going and their eye health is paramount, so clear the excess hair away from the eyes. Cleaning the eyes is very important. The best thing on the market for cleaning eyes inside and out without harming the delicate workings of the eye ball and second eye lid is pure organic Aloe Vera gel, whole leaf. Aloe Vera gel will soften the crusties and remove some of the staining on the hair and make the eyes clean and clear by helping to remove foreign objects from under the second eye lid and soothe the irritated eye ball at the same time.

On a fresh clean cotton pad scoop a dollop of Aloe and gently wipe it across the eye, inside corner to outside corner to clean a normal eye. If there are crusties built up on the inside corners press the Aloe covered cotton pad to the crusty first then wipe down following the tear stain. Keep wiping till the crusty loosens off and then toss cotton pad in the garbage. Get a fresh cotton pad with another dollop of Aloe and carefully clean foreign objects out of the eye and out from under the second eyelid by putting Aloe into the eye and gently moving the lid around and then gently wiping away anything that comes to the edge of the lids or corners of the eyes. The eye ball will be clean, clear, remoisten and soothed by the Aloe Vera Gel.

To naturally kill the bacteria and remove almost all of the red tear stains **under** the eye use tea tree oil on a Q-tip and wipe the area clean. **Do Not** put tea tree oil in the eyes.

Lift the chin straight up to extend the neck and tighten the throat skin and chest area. Carefully run the clippers from chin to base of the throat. Be sure to stretch any loose throat skin sideways to prevent clipper nicks or chunking of hair or skin. Trim hair under chin and blend back to ears and blend into chest. Next, brush muzzle hair forward towards the nose. Wrap your hand gently around the muzzle trim hair using the nose as your guideline. Style the hair around the nose, to suit the client's face or, at the owner's specifications. Circle, oval, semi-circle, square, rectangle, diamond, triangle, inverted triangle, ice cream cone, which is a semi-circle + inverted triangle together), are just a few of the regular shapes for your client's muzzle.

Keeping in mind you want balance and proportion, the amount of hair proportioned to the size of the client's face. You also want the client to look cute/pretty/handsome or suiting their personality. It's the same as in a human hair salon; your job is to bring out your client's best features. But most of all you want to see the client's eyes. Eye contact is very important when communicating with a dog.

Next lift the upper lip and trim stringy hairs on the upper and lower lips that the client licks into their mouths. This is for sanitary reasons. These hairs carry a continual source of bacteria that smell and they are also red-brown in colour from saliva staining. Trimming these hairs also give the client's muzzle a finished look.

The Body and Legs

Now that the worst is over, (nails and feet), and your client can see again, the body and the legs are next. Start by positioning the client standing, facing away from you. Lower or raise the grooming table so your access to your client is at a comfortable height. Run the clippers with the proper blade number attached, along the spine from neck to tail base, with the hair growth, never against. You now have a nice furrowed guideline to follow. Pick a side and overlapping the clipped section with the edge of your clippers, shave the client in neat easy to see rows from neck to tail base following the natural curves of the body. Do the same on the other side of the body. Go over the same areas again with the clippers to fine tune the cut.

Hind Legs

When clipping the legs always start with the hind legs and bum area first, so the client can sit while your clip the front legs. Have the client standing slightly sideways but still facing away from you. Following the hair growth and the curve of the client's leg, clip in even rows. The length of hair is determined by what blade number you use. Go gently over the lower thigh bone and hock areas. Bumping the clippers roughly over these areas will cause the client to pull back. Blend the leg hair into the trimmed foot hair to finish the whole leg. Lift the opposite leg and tail up together and shave from the inner thigh to foot, then push your clippers right under the belly, past the dog for better clipper access to trim the edge of the stifle joint and leg front. Clip any missed hair even with the rest. Do the same on the other hind leg.

Drop Zone

The bum hair is clipped for sanitary reasons. I call it the DROP ZONE because things that drop have a tendency to get stuck in the hair causing discomfort to client and owner's noses. Some clients don't like you working in that area and tend to sit.

Lift the tail up and out of the way and using a number 10 blade, run the clippers carefully from one inch up the underside of the base of the tail to the curve of the groin in a path straight down, using a combing technique clipping the hair in layers because some client's anal hole protrudes more than others due to anal gland swelling or being intact. And when covered with hair it's better to go lightly to prevent nicks in this tender area. This path is only wide enough for the tail to cover, on clients with pants.

Finally, lift the hind leg up and out from the body and gently clip excess hair and mats from around the penis and vulva area, again for sanitary reasons.

Front Legs and Under Arms

Have the client stand or sit facing you on the table. Adjust the table height so you have good visual access to the dog's front legs and under arm areas. Follow the natural flow of muscle and bone, from shoulder to paw in smooth light strokes of the clippers. A lot of clients don't like the vibration on their bones, so be gentle with the pressure along these areas. No bumping of the clippers on the bones. Hold the paw with your hand gently but firmly, to get long smooth strokes with the clippers from shoulder to ankle. Grasp the elbow with your pointer, tall man and thumb, with the paw resting in your palm or along your forearm. This position prevents pull back and helps to absorb the majority of the clipper vibrations and allows you to quickly clip the front lower leg and paw. Lift the front leg up and gently out like a wing, holding the paw or elbow.

Caution #1: have this area at eye level so you can see properly. Lift leg only shoulder high, or you'll strain the shoulder muscles.

Caution #2: have a cool blade on your clippers, as the skin is very delicate in this area and the client will become very un-co-operative if the blade is hot.

Follow the hair growth, gently running your clippers in arching strokes in the hollow of the arm pit, taking hair shorter with each stroke. This helps prevent nicks and burns or chunks in the skin and allows you to see the folds and hollows of the arm pits as the hair is carefully removed. Glide the clippers along the underside of the front leg to the paw in smooth strokes over the delicate bones. Clip in short curved strokes, on the back of lower paw, from upper cushion to large paw pad. For a clean finished look to the back of the paw and ankle. To reach any hair you've missed on the inside leg, turn the client around so that the opposite leg is towards you, lift that leg up. This will expose the inside leg you were working on. Reach under the client's chest and trim missed hair. Always trim down towards the paw. Blend leg hair into trimmed paw hair.

Tails and Ears

The tail is your client's pride and extended vocal cords. The tail tells you what mood they are in and it needs to move and flow to emphasize these moods.

Start by slicing through any mats length wise and brushing them out. Hold the tail straight out, level or slightly lower than the spine. Using a small slicker brush, gently brush the hair backwards, starting at the base of the tail and working your way to the tip, using quick gentle brush strokes to remove any small mats, loose hair or tangles.

Using curved scissors trim hair length to suit style or owner's requests. Make sure you shake the tail so the hair falls differently and trim the long strands. You can fine tune the look of the tail after the bath and drying process.

For the ears, lift the ear leather and smell the ear shell area. Your client's ears should smell musky sweet. If the ear shell smells strong and harsh or rank there is something wrong.

Take a clean cotton pad with a dollop of Aloe Vera gel and clean the inside ear leather and the burr area (the hills and valleys inside the ear shell). Use a Q-tip with Aloe Vera to clean your smaller client's burr area. **DO NOT** use the Q-tip in the ear canal as anything lodged in the canal could be pushed down further. When the cotton becomes soiled change it for a clean one with Aloe Vera. Clean the inside ear leather as well to remove dirt and wax that accumulates there. The Aloe Vera breaks up the dirt and wax nicely.

For clients that require **plucking** all you need is fine talcum powder, your pointer and thumb. Powder the ear hair generously, the powder will absorb the ear wax and moisture and allows for a good grip on the hair by the thumb and finger. Take **small, small** amounts of hair and pull straight up and out quickly from the burr area and ear canal. Move the hair around to break up the clump that sometimes forms by the wax and keep plucking small amounts at a time. Any hair that has grown down the ear canal will be pulled up by the plucking of the other hair.

Sometimes crusties come up from the canal attached to the hair. Make a note of it and inform the owner what you have found. This could be the reason the client can't seem to hear or why the client kept shaking its head or scratching its ear and also the reason for the smell. Recommend a vet check the ears.

Next brush the hair on top of the ear leather, remove any mats. If the ear hair is naturally short comb the hair backwards from base to tip of ear to remove loose hair. Trim ear hair length, to suit the facial structure of the client or follow the owner's request. Thin out heavy looking ears with clippers for a layered look.

The Belly and Groin Areas

Turn the client to face you. Hold both front feet in one hand and lift the client up high on its hind feet. Check your blade for coolness, and clip the belly hair from under arms to groin area, taking care around nipples, vulva, penis, and tender inside flank and groin skin. The inside hind legs and stifle joints can also be clipped from this position. The blade should barely touch the skin and **always follow the natural growth of the hair while clipping, never against.** Blend the hair into the outside flank and rib areas. Set your client back on all fours and praise them. Tell them it's break time and don't go too far away because they still have to have a bath. Put them on the floor to shake and to socialize with the other clients in the Salon.

You take this time to clean up your work area, shake out the towel of excess hair and put it in the towel bin, brush hair off the table, sweep the floor then reset you're grooming table for your next client, as you'll be moving over to the drying table after the bath. Take a washroom break or have some water.

The Wash Cycle

Properly lift the dog into the tub. Have two lanyards available to tie the dog to the tub wall, loosely, if they have a tendency to jump out on you and or sit in the dirty, soapy water.

Turn the water on to a warm comfortable temperature. Dogs, like humans prefer a warm shower. In the summer I have found the slightly colder shower cools the hot dogs down and warmer in the winter stops the shivering in the tub all the time. If the water temperature is uncomfortable on your hands and inner forearm, then it's the same for the dog. Common sense rules here.

So, that said, start with the ears, hold each one flat like a canopy over the ear canal and spray down with the shower head. Work the shower water from head to tail soaking hair thoroughly as you go. With your free hand, move the water through the hair to ensure a thorough saturation. Work water down each leg, under arms and belly and groin areas. Soak water thorough the tail and bum area, all the time following the natural growth of the hair.

Shampoo application begins, again, at the canopied ears. Work the shampoo into the ear hair and it will work its self around to the underside hair without getting into the ear canal. Squirt shampoo around the back of the neck then a little on your free hand and work the low lather around the neck and under the ears and along the chin/muzzle. Using your thumbs move the lather up onto the hair on the nose. Stay a good inch and a half away from the eyes. On a Shih Tzu style face clean the front of the pushed up muzzle. The eye area should have been cleaned while still on the grooming table.

Next squeeze shampoo from the neck to tail base and work into hair. Squeeze shampoo into sides, belly and underarms, gently working it in as you go. Squeeze shampoo down each leg and between the pads of each foot. Set the shampoo bottle aside and using your thumb gently but firmly work the shampoo between the pads. The dog will love the massage of your thumb between the toes. I've had many spread their toes before I even start to rub because it feels good to sore, tired little paws. So don't scrimp on this little pleasure for the dog. They'll stand better for you next time because they know what to expect. Besides who wants to have stale popcorn smelling feet in front of and behind their noses?

Work the shampoo into the top of the paw and up the leg using a cupped circular motion of your palm. Do this with each leg. Squirt shampoo along the tail and using squishing movements with your free hand work the suds into the base, all the way to the tip. Shampoo the bum, vulva and penis areas thoroughly. Set the shampoo bottle aside and with the dog facing you, work the shampoo thoroughly throughout its body and down its legs and belly, always working with the natural growth of the hair, head to tail. Use the pads of your finger tips and give the hair and skin a good firm scrub for two to four minutes, depending on the size and how dirty the dog is. Dogs, like humans, enjoy a good scrub during their shampoo.

Rinse Cycle

Using the same water temperature you started with, rinse the shampoo out starting with the canopied ears again. Use your thumb to move the hair around and loosen the suds. When the ear doesn't feel slimy and the hair squeaks when your rub it, you have rinsed it well. Move on to the other ear, then the neck and chin. Then direct the water flow straight down the spine slowly, moving the hair around by tunnelling your fingers into the wet hair from neck to tail keeping the line of soap suds ahead of the water flow. (Suds in the lead, your hand second, moving water and suds towards the tail and water flow third, closest to the head.) This is the quickest, most efficient way to rinse shampoo out of the hair using gravity and the water flow with gentle agitation to help move it along.

Do the same technique along the sides and down each leg and down the chest area. Next rinse the tail and bum area thoroughly. Then rinse the inside legs and arm pits, belly and groin areas last because if you follow the natural path of the water these areas are where the rinsed soap, from the top of the dog, ends up. You rinse this area last. When the top of the dog is rinsed squeaky clean and believe me, you'll hear the hair squeak as you run your fingers through the well rinsed areas, you'll know if you missed any spots because they will be slimy or slippery to the touch. So, rinse the under carriage of the dog last and thoroughly.

Using the same basic procedure as for the small dogs, large dogs are not that hard to wash. The only thing different is that you do half of the dog at a time. Wet half of the dog, then, turn the dog around using the swing turn and wet the other half. Wash half the dog, swing, wash the other half, rinse that half, then swing and rinse the other half and so on.

Most dogs only have to have one shampoo if you scrub them properly. Some dogs will need to be spot cleaned in the second shampoo. For example, lower legs, under arms or belly because of mud etc. You only need to shampoo that area again, not the whole dog, till that area is squeaky clean like the rest of the dog.

Outdoor or farm dogs or dogs that roll in a wonderful scent will need that second full shampoo to get everything out. There are certain breeds you can't get away with only one shampoo, Cocker Spaniels for example because of the excess oil in their very fine thick coats. Use your eyes, nose and touch to determine if you need to spot clean or go for the full second shampoo. Don't be lazy, do it right the first time.

Conditioner

Pump a blob of conditioner into your hand and rub your palms together. Once again, start at the ears and lightly slide them through your hands, leaving a skiff of conditioner on them. Next, move to the tail and squeeze in the rest from base to tip. Pump another blob into your palm, rub your hands together and glide your hands over the entire body and down the legs distributing the conditioner evenly over the hair. Run your hands and fingers over the entire body again and work the conditioner into the hair. You know when you`ve missed a spot because the hair feels rough. Apply conditioner to the missed spots. Comb the bum pants and leg feathers with your fingers to distribute conditioner thoroughly through them and apply more conditioner where needed. Different hair types and lengths require different amounts of conditioner. Common sense rules here.

Final Rinse Cycle

Quickly and thoroughly rinse the conditioner off the dog`s hair, following the head to tail gravity flow, belly and inner legs last. The conditioner will also help remove any residual shampoo, clinging loose hairs and dander etc. You will feel the difference in the hair before and after you condition and rinse.

Using your hands like a squeegee, start at the ears and work down the neck, chest and front legs in long smooth strokes, slicking the excess water off the dog`s body. Then squeegee the back, chest, belly and down the back legs, then squeeze water from the base of the tail to the tip.

Next hold a towel under your chin and pick the small to medium size dog up against your chest and wrap one end of the towel around the front of the dog and the other end around the back and bum of the dog so that it is entirely covered by the towel except its head. The dog is warm and the towel absorbs more water. Then head to the drying table.

For a large dog, after slicking the excess water off, put a towel on the floor and drape another over the entire dog. Guide the dog to the edge of the tub and help them out on to the floor. The larger dog walks around the bathing room shaking the excess water out. The more water the dog shakes out the less work you`ll have to do in the drying process. You follow it around with sham-wow type towels to absorb and rub the dog down from head to all four feet, which prepares the dog for...

Drying

Believe it or not, drying a large dog is a bit hazardous for the groomer, especially when using the ultimate drying tool, the Master Blaster. An eight horse power drying machine that uses ambient air and cuts your drying time to a quarter of the time it usually takes with other drying methods, drying kennels, air drying, stand dryers etc. The first drawback is that it`s loud. After blasting three large dogs dry in one day, I felt like I`d been to the night club dancing beside the speakers. My ears were getting numb. Plus with the hair blown off the dogs and around the room during drying I kept getting hair in my eyes and had to stop to clean them out. So I made my way quickly to the work safety equipment store after work and bought three pairs of safety glasses and three pairs of ear protectors. I don`t care what I look like while I`m drying the dogs because I can still see and hear. The dog doesn`t care what I look like, as long as he gets dried quickly, to prevent a chill, he`s a happy camper and so am I.

The other sets of protection gear are for the owners who come to watch or help hold the dog for me so I have an extra pair of hands to work with.

Please note that dog`s ears are designed with muscles to close off the ear canal from loud noises and water while swimming etc. Just like their second eyelid for visual protection. Mother Nature is wonderful that way!

So, back to drying the large dog, safety protection in place, lanyard around the dog`s neck and one around the lower belly and attach these two lanyards together to make a holder to prevent the dog from sitting or lying down and to keep him in place by your side. Turn on the first switch of the blaster and aim the hose at the back hip area about four inches from the hair. Move the hose back and forth in long even lines along the dog`s back and hip areas. Keep the hose moving constantly along the dog`s body, do not leave the blaster blowing on one spot too long. You`ll see your progress by the hair the blaster moves. Praise the dog for standing still. When he`s use to the noise and the feel of the blowing nozzle, flip the second switch on for the full 8 horse power, then watch the fur fly, as well as the excess water from the hair.

Most dogs will stand very well for the blaster as long as you stay behind the ears and blast the hair in horizontal and vertical sweeps moving towards the tail following the natural growth of hair. Some dogs will allow their ears and head to be blown dry at half-speed. Others prefer the very quiet stand dryer or towel drying on their head and ears.

Ok, dry the back, sides, outer legs, bum and tail, then the belly and inner leg, following the water gravity flow pattern as in bathing. This is the quickest, most efficient way to dry a large dog. Use horizontal and vertical lines to blast off the water from neck to tail especially for longer haired dogs to prevent tangling. Send the dog into the grooming room to relax, socialize with the other dogs or do his business outside. While the large dog relaxes you get to take a small break, drink some water etc. then squeegee the floor of water and wet hair, pick up towels and rinse the tub. Then head into the grooming room for the fine tuning. These breaks are for the benefit of both you and the dog. They are only two to three minutes long but you each get to regroup and it helps you both to stay calm.

We left off with the small to medium size dog, wet, bundled up in a towel and being carried to the drying table. Place the dog on the drying table. Slip the lanyards into place and loosely close the toggles. Remove the towel and rub excess water from the hair. Most dogs really love to be scrubbed with the towel, rubbing their faces and heads into it and dancing around on the table. Throw the wet towel in the towel bin and set up the stand dryer. Use high heat in the fall and winter, medium to low heat in spring and summer. **Note hair in the winter is thicker and longer, this means drying time will be longer than in the spring and summer. Book your appointment time according to season and drying times needed.**

Have the dog stand facing away from you. Start at the back of the neck, dry the hair straight down the spine. Using only your hands to move the hair up and out to allow the water to quickly travel off the hair shaft. Turn the dog to face left or right so you can dry one entire side thoroughly starting at the back leg and bum area and then side and under belly, front leg and chest, working around to the other side using the same pattern, back leg and bum, side and under belly, front leg and chest areas. Lastly, the head, muzzle then the ears. If the hair stays wet in clumps, use a small slicker brush to lightly break up the clumps. **Don't touch the skin with the slicker brush, only the clumps of hair.** As the dryer blows the hair dry, keep your hands moving through the air flow of the dryer, so the dog's skin does not heat up from the continual blowing in one spot. Systematically move the blower nozzle position along the dog's body as the hair becomes dry. Raise and lower the drying table to aid the dryer process with better angles and access to belly, groin and inner leg areas.

When the small, medium and large size dogs are thoroughly dried, the dogs are ready for fine tuning.

Fine Tuning

Fine tuning is giving the dog's hair a final once over with the scissors, trimming stray hairs between the toes and pads of the feet, on the tail, legs muzzle chin and ears. The hair gets a final brushing to remove any loose hair, small tangles and to smooth the hair into place.

Final Touches

Final touches are the most important tool to finish off your clients new do. They are clips, fancy ear ribbons or colourful bandana. I hold up a folded pile of colourful bandanas and ask the dog which colour they want. Many have picked their own colour by touching the colour with their nose, by licking the colour of choice, touching the colour with their paw or rooting through the various colours and grabbing their choice with their teeth.

I have found that, contrary to popular belief, dogs are **NOT** colour blind and my clients have proven over and over again that they can see colours and the colours they choose compliment their hair colour beautifully. I should call Myth Busters and let them know about this busted myth.

Anyways, roll the bandana down to fit the size of the dog's neck, tie a reef knot, left over right and under, and right over left and under. This is a nice looking knot. Tuck the ends into the bandana and slide the points towards the front for a tidy look. Remove the dog's collar from the grooming arm and let the dog smell the collar before you put it back on him. The dog will nudge, smell or lick the collar in acknowledgement of its own scent. Attach the collar to the dog's neck turning the collar so the tags hang down over the bandana point. Unhook the lanyards from the dog's body, pick the dog up properly and set him on the floor, patting his side a few times gently and tell him "good boy/girl all done". The dog will shake, go admire himself in the mirror or go and show off to the other dogs. Clean up and reset the work area for the next client.

Nails, never be afraid to trim them

A lot of Groomers and Owners are afraid to trim dog nails, especially the black ones because they cut them too short, hit the quick and the dog is bleeding and in pain. Fussing, whining, yipping, struggling and biting begins because...damn it, it hurts!! Plus dogs do remember exactly which nail was cut too short because they are cool and calm with the other nails being trimmed and suddenly start to fuss and pull back over one nail.

So from this paragraph on read carefully more than once because this is how to trim nails **without** pain or blood all the time!

First of all, pull the hair back off the nail area and really look at the nails. Notice the following:

1. The colour of the nails.
2. The length of the nails.
3. Where is the quick?
4. Is the quick even or uneven throughout **all** the nails? (Yes, even the black ones too, keep reading and the secret to the black nails will be revealed!!)
5. Check the angle of wear on the nail tips this indicates the way the dog walks off its pads and onto the nail.
6. Check for broken nails.
7. If there is a broken nail, check for inflammation or tenderness around the nail bed and toe.
8. Check for dew claws on all four feet, this check is very important because...
9. Some dew claws and some nails will curve and grow into the toe pad causing a lot of pain and infections. Finally,

10. Watch the dog's response to this quick but thorough inspection. Do they pull back their paws? Do they table dance and start to twist? Do they snap? If so, be prepared to muzzle the dog while you work on the nails and feet trimming, for both your protection.

This inspection takes very little time and is very important because the feet are the dog's foundation and can make or break pain in the rest of the dog's body. Ask anyone with sore feet where they hurt because they are compensating for those sore tootsies?

The dog will let you know the nails are too long by the ticking on the floor, by the rusty orange lick spots on the toes and lower legs and feet or the dog will chew their nails because they are too long.

Nail Colour

There are five colours of nails, black, white, burgundy, striped black and white and striped burgundy and white. These stripes are vertical and follow the nail shape from nail bed to tip.

Black Nails

We'll start with the worst colour first, Black. Owners, Vets and Groomers alike hate cutting the black nails because they can't see the quick. Ahh, but take another look, the quick **is** visible, really.

Take a good look at the black nail. For the moment, ignore the quick inside the nail. Look at the outside of the black nail closely. The nail coming from the nail bed is nice and smooth, shiny even. Then the nail starts to look scored and dull towards the tip. This is your demarcation line. This line is jagged and uneven but it does circle around the black nail. Some are very faint but it will still be there around the nail.

Cut the nail **below** the lowest point on the demarcation line. That is the safe zone on a black nail, because the quick is in the shiny half. Turn the toe so you can see the bottom of the cut nail, can you see a **small** round circle in the center of the nail? If so do not cut any more as that is the beginning of the quick, the smaller the center circle the safer the quick is. The bigger the center circle in the nail, the closer and more painful you are to bleeding the quick. **Be very careful.** If there is no **small** center circle in the nail tip and it is all white trim the nail in thin increments till you can see the **small** center circle.

Hold it!! Now before you start blissfully trimming all the black nails in site you will find that the odd dog will have this in the reverse. That odd dog will have the scoring coming from the nail bed and the smooth shiny black on the tips. The same cut still applies. Cut **below** the demarcation line.

Hold on hold on, there is one more type of black nail that is really different. It's the totally black shiny nail with a white tip at the end. Cut **only** the white tip because the quick is really long. The white tip is the old nail that the colour has leached out, because it grew past the nourishing quick.

Ok, now you can safely cut all the black nails you could ever want!

White, Black and White, Burgundy, Burgundy and White Nails

On all of these nail colours, the rule of thumb is to look at the **side** of the nail before you cut, to see where the quick rests because the quick will be deceiving on some dogs nails. The quick will extend further out along the bottom of the nail then at the top. That's the reason you end up making the easy white nails bleed because you are going by the top of the nail not the bottom. So you will have to cut further down the tip by using an angle **\\,** (back slash) way past the start of the solid white in order to miss the angled quick. This angle **** cut encourages the quick to recede on the bottom by removing the protective top part of the nail. It will take two or three trims on this angle to correct the growth of the quick so that you are then able to make a, **I** vertical cut and keep the nails short.

Some white nails are only white at the very tip of the nail because the quick is so far down the nail that the entire nail looks pink. Only trim the white tip but cut it on a **** (back slash) angle.

These angles are used to correct and recede the quick evenly in every nail. The quick will recede back up the nail and allow more nail tip to be cut off next trimming. Some dogs only need to have this angling done one or two times, some dogs need it done more to encourage the quick to recede.

Ok, I have to add another type of nail to this list because I had a new client come to my salon twice now and low and behold this dog's nails were banded **horizontally!!** All the striped nails I've done were vertical. This dog's nail bands were black and cream and black and burgundy and only ¼ inch wide bands of colours. So I checked the sides of the nails and yes you could see the quick and I found that I only had to cut one band of colour on each of the nails. I have only seen this dog twice in the last two years.

Is this a new self-preservation evolution for dogs? The body pre-marks the nails so silly humans only cut one band at a time to prevent pain and bleeding? We can only dream. Until that time, save the dogs the pain and learn to trim their nails properly.

How often should the nails be trimmed?

Ok folks, this is the answer that every Groomer and Vet should be telling the owners: You need to trim your dog's nails every three to four weeks depending on how fast they grow. In the spring time your dog's nails suddenly, overnight become eagle talons. This is because your dog is reducing the energy needed to stay warm, especially in Canada, and increasing the energy in the regenerative areas, nails and summer coat regrowth. Some of my clients come in every two weeks in the spring because the nails grow so fast. So literally play it by ear, when you hear the ticking on the floor it's time for a nail trim. Or lift the dog's paw up like a horses hoof. Do the nails extend past the toe pad? Yes? Then they need to be trimmed. The nails, looking at them in profile, should sit half way down the toe pad. This stops the ticking on the floor, foot pain etc. and still allows dig in when the dog runs.

Small to Medium dogs

The best way to trim small to medium dogs nails is on the grooming table. Have the owner remove the leash. Lift the dog properly onto the table. Raise or lower the table to a comfortable height. Start with the right front paw, then the left front paw then the left hind paw and the right hind paw. Be sure to check and trim the dew claws. **Do not cut any nails if the dog is pulling back its leg or dancing around the table.** Triple strap the dog (two lanyards and a collar to the grooming arm), in this case to safely prevent excess movement of the dog then proceed with the trimming. Or have the owner snug the dog's head in the crook of their elbow and the dog's body snug across their chest while you trim their nails. Another way is to hook your finger into the dog's collar and hold the paw in the same hand. This allows absolutely no pull back and the dog seems to calm down quickly.

Some dogs are more comfortable with these ways of trimming because they can't see. When trimming the stressed dog, calmly, using voice inflection, praise the dog after each nail has been trimmed. Do not let the paw go. Hold on to the paw and gently rub the toe you just trimmed, between your thumb and finger of your free hand. Move on to the next toe nail trim and praise. This retraining method shows the dog that every time they hold still they get praised when the nail is trimmed. The dog will build up its confidence and trust in you as their pedicurist and eventually just sit or stand while their nails are trimmed. Yes, they will because I have a whack load of nail clients that fussed, fought, bit etc.

because they'd been hurt by others during previous nail trims and now they just stand or sit while I trim their nails.

Trimming Larger Dog Nails

Strap on your knee pads and have the owner sit in a comfy chair. Have the dog sit in front of the owner. Take the leash off. The owner holds the collar, keeping the muzzle up and scrubs the chest area slowly and calmly. Using the same pattern, right front left front etc. leave the feet on the floor and trim the tips below the quick. Open the trimmers wide to go around the nail on the floor. This method allows proper trimming and ensures space between the nails and the floor. No ticking, no pain and no bleeding. Also there is less stress and fighting with a large strong dog that pulls back its paw.

So large dogs keep four on the floor for nail trimming or they can lie down or sit as you lift each paw to be trimmed. Read the dog and apply the method that suits.

Nail trimming should take no more than three minutes tops, fighting and dancing included. Because it only takes a short time, nail trimming should be a walk-in service, no appointment necessary.

Groomers nail trimming is a **necessity for dogs.** Don't over price something that is so important to a dog's health and physical mobility. No more than $11.00 dollars should be charged on this vital service. You know what to look for in all the nail colours and how to trim them properly. You have no excuse to neglect the nails or cut them too short. Eleven dollars every three weeks over a year will net you a nice profit for only three minutes of you time. Everybody wins in the end. The dog gets a nice pain and blood free nail trimming on a regular basis, the owner's wallet isn't gouged, which will encourage the owner to bring the dog back more often. It's quick, clean, no pain, no blood and the dogs in and out again and you get a regular nail client.

Sedation to Trim Nails?!!

What?! If you have to sedate the **average** dog to have its nails trimmed, the person trimming the nails is doing it **wrong.** Sedation of any kind is hard on the dog's system, stressful to the owner, not to mention expensive $35.00 to $65.00 to have this type of nail trimming done. What's wrong with this picture? Have that person read this section on the proper way to trim nails or find someone who knows how to trim the nails properly.

Nail Trimmers, Which Style is better?

The best pair of trimmers is a sharp pair. I prefer the scissor style. It allows me to see the entire nail and quick as I am cutting. I use the medium size for all size dogs because they fit comfortably in my hand and allow me to trim quickly. Remove the wire latch that holds the trimmers closed when not in use because it can flip and lock the trimmers while you are trying to cut and it will also pinch your palm as you trim. That hurts.

Some groomers prefer the dremil tool to file the nails down. They are good but you have to be careful because they heat up the nail quickly causing the nail to burn. The same as a dremil tool at a lady's nail salon, they burn. So be careful and check the temperature often and only touch the dremil to the nail in short quick touches to prevent excess heat build-up. Get a dremil that has a variable speed and go slow till you become proficient with this tool.

Black Nails

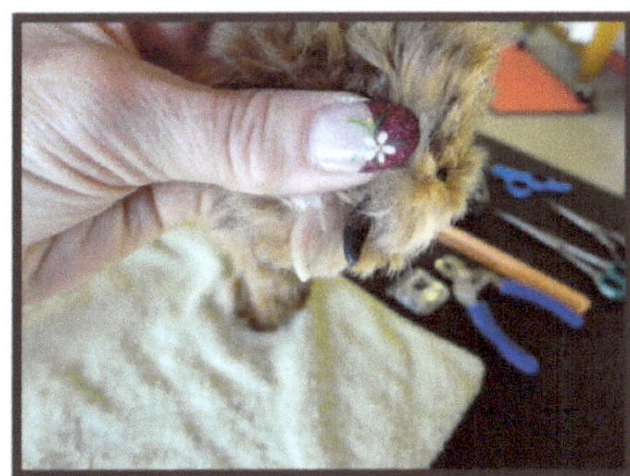

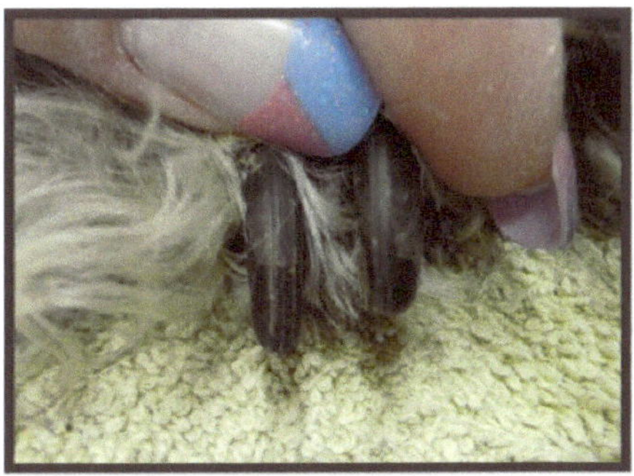

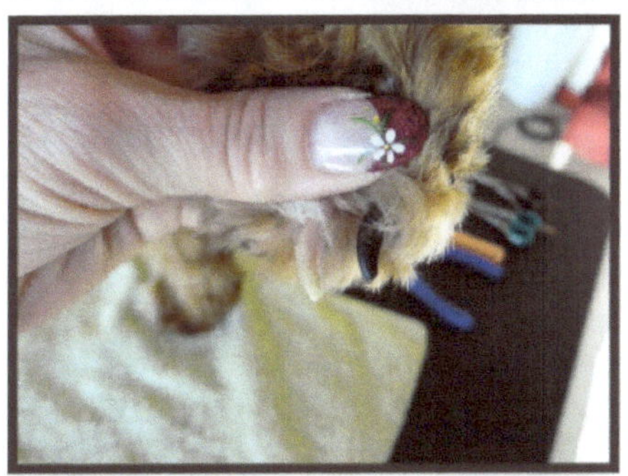

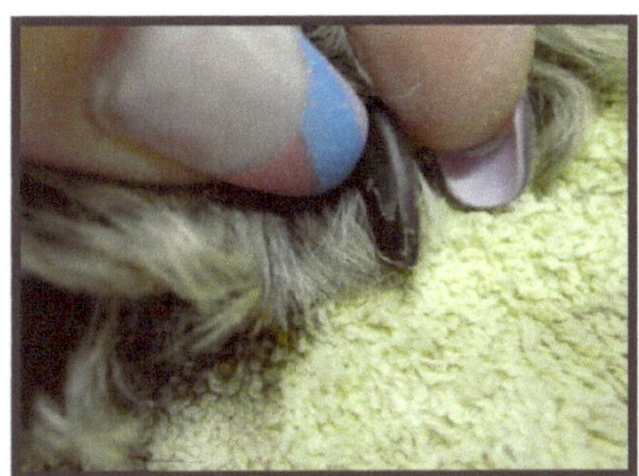

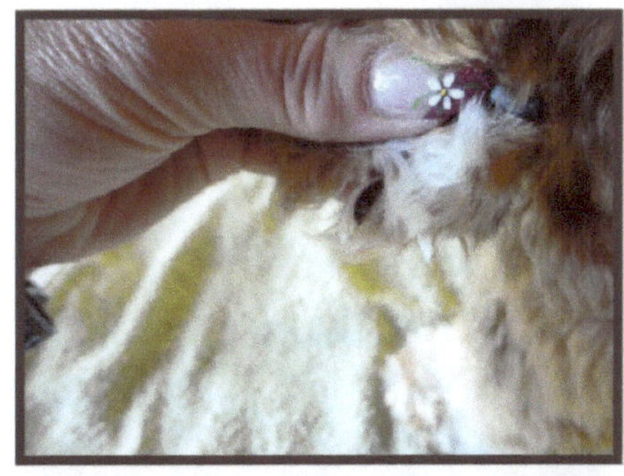

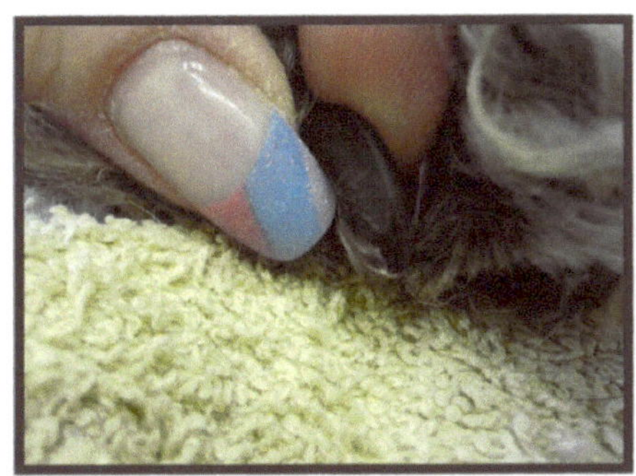

White Nails and Striped Nails

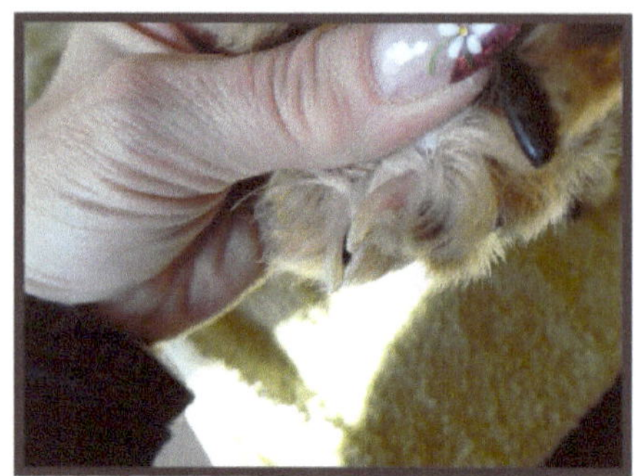

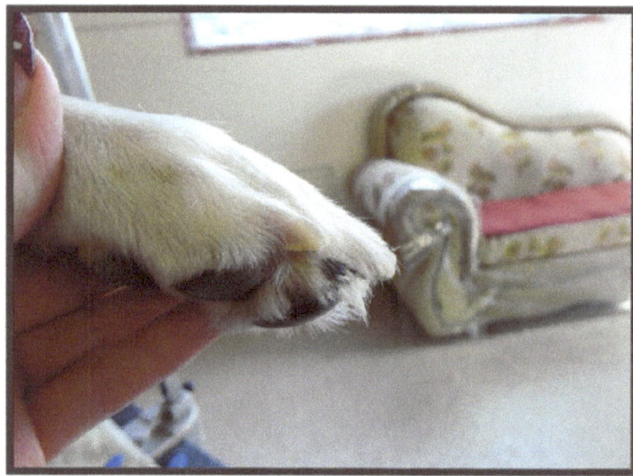

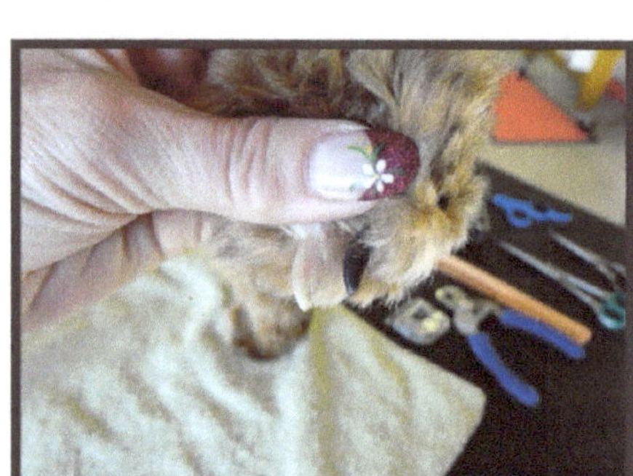

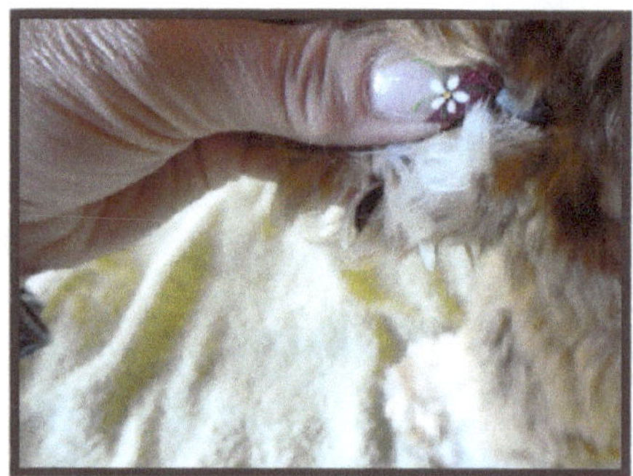

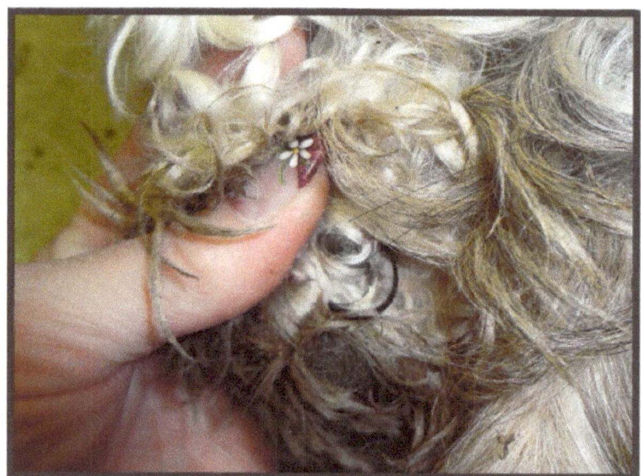

Help My Dog Is Matted

The bane of existence to a dog and their owner is mats. In this chapter, I will discuss the different kinds of mats and how they form, then how to fix them.

Spider Web Mats

Spider web mats are loosely woven mats that tangle on the ends or the middle of the hair shaft and are very painful. These tangles create long and short hair lengths. The mat, close to the skin, looks like the outside edges of a spider web, uneven, because it's attached to various objects. The pain comes into play by the short hairs pulling the skin because the long hairs allow the mat to move around. Spider web matting comes in combination with blanket matting. They can be all over the body or as single painful mat in the groin and belly area and behind the ears. Spider web mats can tear areas of skin off if the mats are heavy enough and create a red pulled area, both can lead to hot spots and infection. I've seen this happen to ears, groin and bum areas.

Blanket Mats

Blanket matting is dense thick matting in various heights from "easy for the clippers to get underneath" height to the "close to the skin sunlight can't reach" height where you have to split the mat carefully to the skin with a pair of scissors to get it started because the clippers can't even break through.

These mats are compounded greatly by groomers or owners thinking if they bath the dog and use conditioner the mats will loosen. **Wrong!** The mats react like sheep's wool and shrink, shrink, shrink, creating a bad and very painful situation for the dog.

Blanket matting can happen all over the dogs body and when shaved down with # 7 or more often than not a # 10 blade, the mat shaved off will look like sheep's wool or a pelt in the shape of the dog. Blanket matting can be in combination with spider web matting. Blanket matting can be caused by two or more textures of hair, dry course hair, dry candy floss hair or soft downy hair that falls out in tufts like goose down. These three hair types in a combination are the worst for blanket matting.

To split these mats to the skin carefully use a short blade pair of scissors, 5" to 6" in length and snip a hole into the top of the mat. Spread it apart, snip your way carefully down to the skin. When the skin is finally exposed, slide the scissor blade along the skin under a small section of mat and cut the hole in a straight line along the area you are de-matting. For example the body, follow the spine. The leg, start at the top of the leg and carefully snip your way down in a straight line to the foot or the end of the mat.

When your line is complete spread the matted hair apart and using #7 or #10 blades, carefully clip one side of the matted area and then the other side till the mat is totally removed. Sometimes you have to continue using scissors and clippers to break the mats up to remove them.

Caution #1: Remember to snip and clip carefully because if the blanket matting is combined with spider web matting it can be painful to the dog because hairs and skin are being pulled.

Caution #2: Sores, hot spots and possible infections could be lurking under blanket matting, especially because the mats are so dense, it will hold water, sweat, dirt, twigs, thorns burrs, etc. All will irritate already sensitive skin not to mention being imbedded into the skin as well. So peel back that matting gently and carefully.

Friction Mats

Friction matting is pretty straight-forward, it is caused by the body parts moving back and forth over certain areas of the body knotting the hair up in that area.

Friction matting happens in the groin area, inside hind legs, front underarms, and the bum area and under the tail base area caused by straight down tails wagging. The tail that curves over the back, mats at the tip and top of the tail base and mats the back hair in front of the tail base.

The friction mats on the back, tail and bum areas can be split and brushed out easily. The friction mats under the arms, inside hind legs and groin areas need to be shaved with # 10 blade, as the areas are too tender to even think about combing/brushing them out.

Shedding Mats

In the spring and fall is the best time to see shedding mats. They look like tufts of hair sticking out from under the dog's coat and can be easily pulled out. There is ample space underneath them for clippers if the owner requests the dog to be shaved.

Brushing is the best way to quickly remove these mats. If some are too dense to brush, split the mat length wise two or three times then pull them apart with your fingers, then brush what's left out. Use a_small slicker brush to remove the bulk of the mats then use a rake to remove the rest of the loose hair. Line brushing and raking is the best technique to use for maximum hair removal.

Compression Mats

This type of matting I have found more on larger dogs or older dogs. This type of matting is caused by the dog lying on one side all the time or sitting to one side. When constantly squashed against the ground etc. under the weight of the large/old dog the hair becomes compressed or like a bad case of bed head. The matting is located on one hip or on the side of the dog and can be easily removed by a good brushing.

The hair is thicker on that side or area because it's always on the ground/floor or cement and grows thicker to cushion the bones and for more insulation. The hair on the "sunny side up" will be less dense and a breeze to brush.

Ear Mats

Ear mats whether large or small are very painful to the dog. They are always combination mats, friction mats from petting and scratching and spider web mats. They can be loose or so close to the skin that the spider web matting has pulled pieces of skin off because of the weight of the mats.

I had one dog come in with ear mats that were so huge; I couldn't find his ears because they were matted from the top of the ears all the way around and under the chin and cheeks. *Groomers must be very cautious with the ear tips after removing heavy matting like this. The blood does not circulate properly when matted this badly and will pool at the tips and then will drain out from the tips as the dog shakes its head in relief. **Do not stop the drainage; let nature do its thing.** Do have your camera handy for before, during and after photos for typical C.Y.A.* in this instance.

Use scissors or clippers only if you can see space between the skin and the mat. If the mat is dangerously close to the skin, cut the mat horizontally or width wise to break the spine of the mat. Pull the mat gently apart with your fingers to loosen the denseness then clipper the rest of the mat off. Use whatever mat removal method that causes the least amount of pain to the dog.

Let the dog smell the mat after you remove it from the ear area and scratch the bare spot behind the ear to stimulate the skin and loosen dead skin and hair. Besides it feels good to the dog.

Rule of thumb with mats, take your time and go carefully. They are painful and could be hiding other problems under their denseness. De-matting a dog is time consuming, depending on how matted and how large the dog is. Charge accordingly. *Cover your ass.

To Shave or Not To Shave

I have had owners phone me or come into the salon and say “shave ‘em to the wood”. For the spring and summer. I have also heard the other side of the coin, “you can’t shave that kind of dog, it’ll ruin their coat or my vet said not to shave the dog down”.

Well folks, I hate to point out the obvious but you aren’t the one wearing a fur coat in +30c to +40c heat; the dog is. The owner that has their dog shaved is thinking of their dogs comfort and health in the spring and summer heat. Remember these are **not show dogs,** they are family members and many owners will seek what’s best for their beloved pet.

<u>Fact #1:</u> the hair does grow back just fine, all breeds have been shaved down and the hair grows back properly over and over.

<u>Fact #2:</u> **the only time a coat does not grow back properly is because there is an under lying health problem**, bad teeth, anal gland issues, poor diet, worms, low grade infections, old age. The hair is external and is fed by the blood at its root in the hair follicle. If the blood or body is fighting off health problems the hair growth will take second place. **Remember the hair and nails are the first indicators that something is wrong with the health of an animal.**

<u>Fact #3:</u> the owner is not tripping over hair balls rolling around their house in spring and summer from shedding.

<u>Fact #4:</u> the dog feels cooler and acts younger.

<u>Fact #5:</u> shaving the dog down in the spring will uncover anything out of the normal, for example: sores, hot spots, embedded straw, sticks, thorns etc. any insect infestation, fleas, ticks, lice and yes even maggots in open sores and hotspots.

<u>Fact #6:</u> shaving prevents matting as the winter coat is shed and also helps prevent future matting as the coat grows in because it's easier to brush and maintain for the owner.

Fact #7: owners have fallen in love all over again with their dog after they are shaved down because they look different, cuter and act like a puppy again. Some dogs can't get enough of themselves in the mirrors after being shaved down.

Once again this choice is up to the Owner.

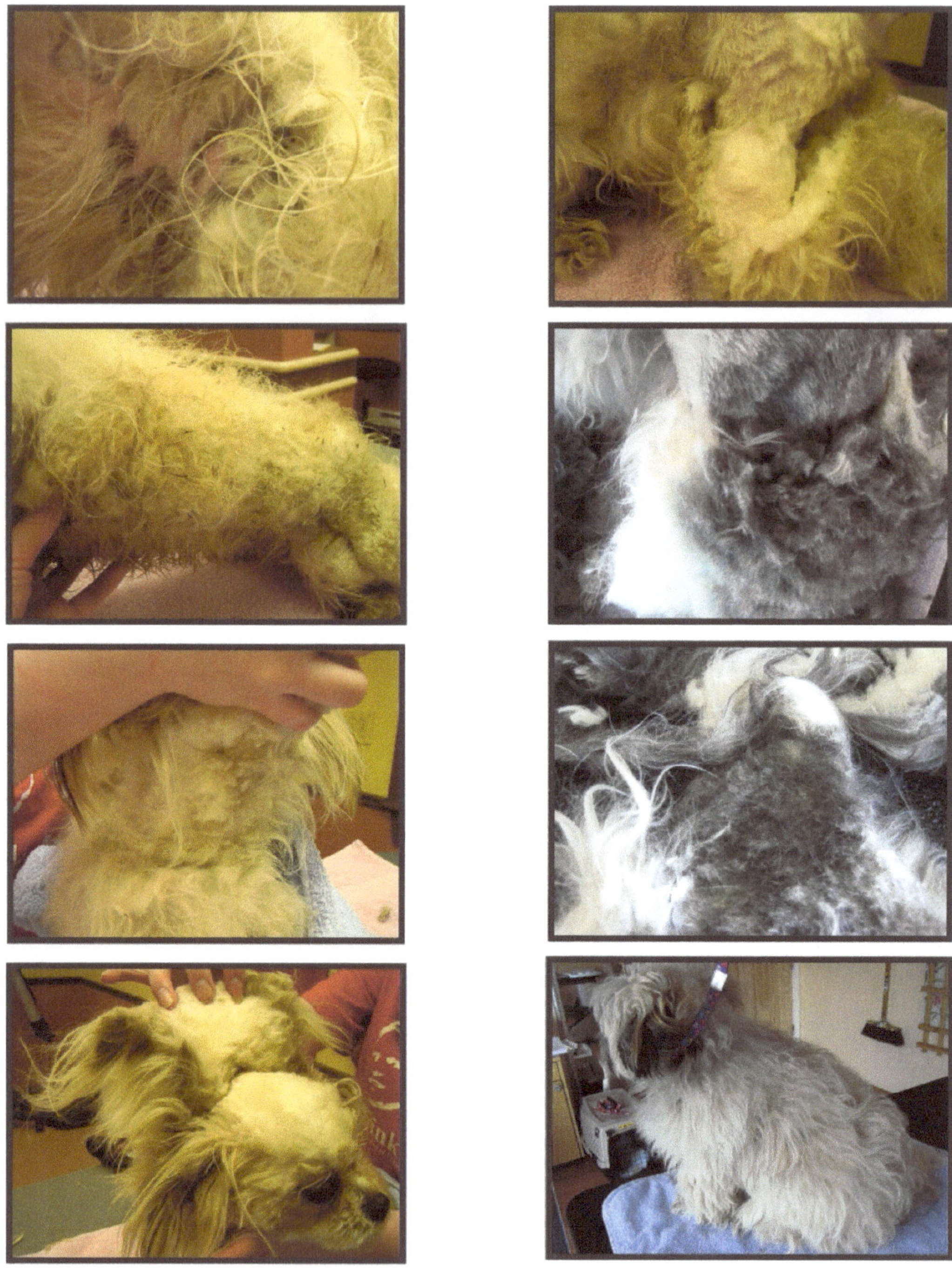

That Extra Scratch Behind the Ear Renaissance grooming

Mats

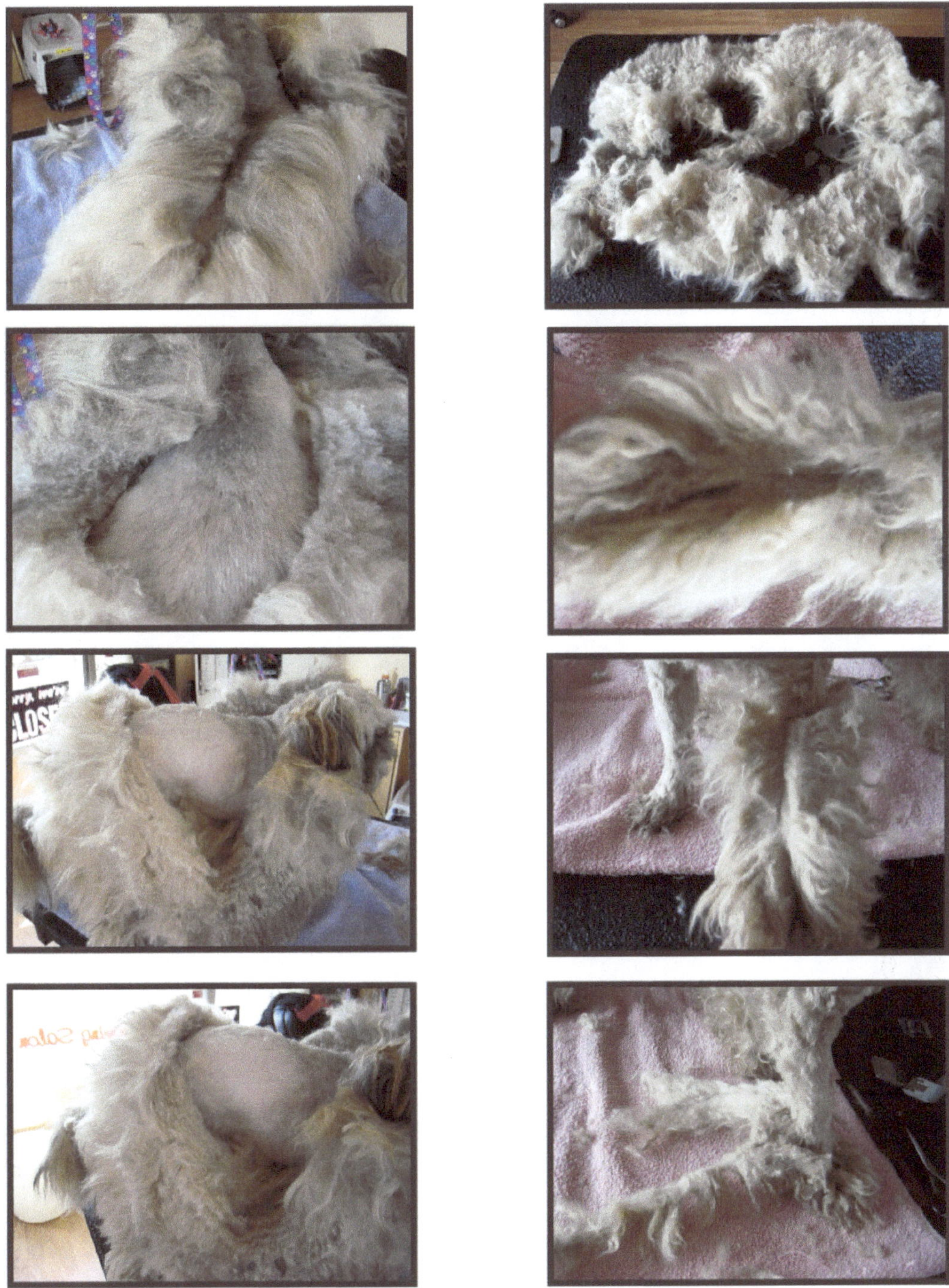

That Extra Scratch Behind the Ear Renaissance grooming

Mats

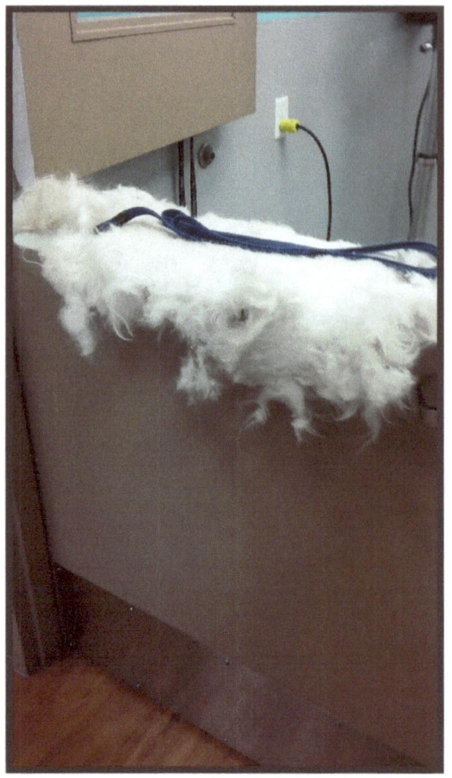

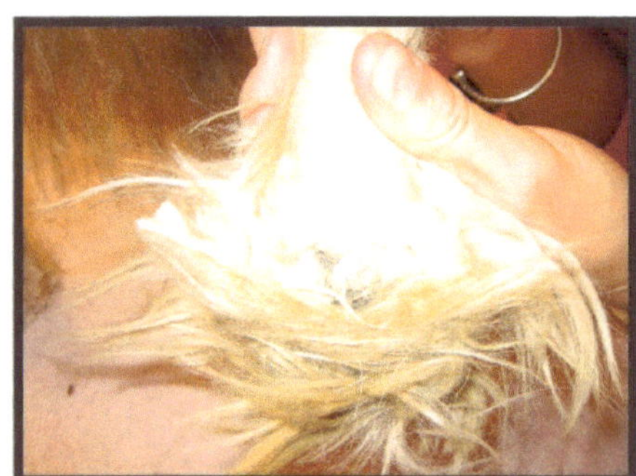

That Extra Scratch Behind the Ear Renaissance grooming

Grooming A Cat Is Easier Than You Think!!

Cats are cool! They are very sensual creatures as well as extremely independent. One must remember that a cat doesn't like to be held too tight, pinned down in any way or held too long. They become upset, cranky, will scratch and bite without hesitation if they figure it'll change their situation.

So, with all this in mind set your table this way: remove the lanyards and grooming arm from the table. Place a towel on the table and have the owner place the cat on the towel and calmly pet the cat. Remove the cat's collar.

The very first thing you do is get rid of the weapons! Quickly trim all of the claws. Have a soft cat muzzle ready just in case the cat has a tendency to bite. If the cat is relaxed don't use it. With the weapons taken care of, you are safe to proceed.

To start the lion cut on a cat, use #7 or 10 blade. Start the clippers at the shoulder blades, in one smooth, straight path from shoulder blades to tail base. Shave one side of the cat in smooth even strips making the path wider and wider with each blade path. You should be able to shave down to a quarter of the belly then start on the other side of the cat. Have the owner lift the cat up, facing away from you, by gently encircling the ribs under the armpits. Keep the hind feet on the towel. Quickly shave any exposed areas in the same smooth paths and blend into back legs and trim bum area.

Have the owner turn the cat around calmly to face you and open their fingers so you can start shaving paths from the underarms/chest all the way down to the groin being careful around the nipples on both male and female cats. Shave the inside legs and any spots you need to go over to remove lines etc. Next put the cat down on all fours and blend the mane into the shorter hair on the back. Blend the shoulder hair into the front legs, then, trim long stringy hair around ears and face and chest to look thicker. Shave the armpit hair for coolness and blend into chest hair. Shave over the back again to remove lines and hair you missed.

Some owners like the tail to be full, if so, brush the hair on the tail backwards with the small slicker and then blend the base of the tail into the short hair.

Some owners like the tail shaved with only a whip on the end, it makes a portable toy for the cat. When the shaving is complete, get a hot wet towel and wipe the shaved bits, dead hair, dirt and dander off the cat's coat. 99.99% of cats hate being bathed so don't even go there unless you want to unclamp that same cat from your arm. Been there, done that, and had to get the Tetanus shot! 100% of the cats I have wiped down with a hot wet towel did not fuss at all. They seem to enjoy the warmth. Clean the ears,tie a bandana around their neck, reattach the collar and place the cat back in its carrier.

Sedate The Cat?! Are You Nuts?!!

Within one week I had four separate cat owners call my salon asking me if I sedated the cat before I groomed. I told the owners no, that cats do not need to be sedated to be groomed. That sedation was very hard on any animal. All the owners were very relieved to hear this and booked appointments for their cats after I explained that a cat can be groomed within 45 minutes, no sedation involved, the cat is held gently and petted by the owner while I worked quickly and efficiently shaving the cat to order.

Rule of Thumb: if you are scared, angry or stressed you become tense. The animals will know and pick up on it and reflect it back in behaviour.

Stay calm. Your breathing is the key. Take breaks, eat and drink fluids on a regular basis, listen to calm relaxing music and maintain a comfortable room temperature while you work.

Problem Solving

Front Leg Puller/Twitcher

Twitcher are dogs who twitch their paw or whole leg at the slightest touch of the scissors just a small enough movement, constantly to make it hard to trim around the toes safely. Hold the paw firmly but gently in your free hand, brace your elbow against your side and lock it there. This almost eliminates this excess, annoying movement.

Pullers are dogs that pull their paw straight back constantly or at the last second before you trim the nail or trim the feet hair. Hold the dogs elbow between your pointer, tall man and thumb. Lock your elbow again at your side. If the dog has had lots of experience doing this movement retraining is needed to stand, stay and hold. For now turn him sideways and lift the paw like a horses hoof and trim the nails. Or hook a finger from the hand holding the paw into the neck lanyard. This holds the paw in place for you to trim the nail.

Hind Leg Kickers

Dogs who kick back like mules when you touch their hind pads. Use the elbow lock or for extreme kickers brace the hock against the grooming arm pole and hold it there gently but firmly while you cut around and between the pads. This prevents the back kick and allows you to safely work around the pads.

Biters

For both yours and the dog's safety, muzzle biters a.s.a.p. When the dog snaps or bites at you even with the muzzle reprimand with a firm **No Teeth.** I have had quite a few dogs back down from biting just by tapping their fang and looking them in the eye and saying **No Teeth** then, still looking them in the eye I lift my lip and tap my much larger fang and say **No Teeth.** Most settle down after that. The persistent ones are in constant retraining. Some will settle down once they know you are not going to hurt them and the muzzle comes off, usually after the feet are done. The final few who need lots of retraining, the muzzle stays on and is only removed when doing the face. After the face is done the muzzle is back on for the bath and drying.

For the dog that snaps at you when you go to pick them up, this is a fear biter afraid you are going to hurt them. Throw a towel over them and quickly pick them up. They usually settle down when in your arms and on the table. **Safety first, for both of you.**

Face Pullers

These are the dogs that pull their face either at the last second as you are about to snip or clip around the eyes, one side or the other on the face, usually the snub nose style faces. There is a very high risk of injury when the dog does this move.

a. Lower the table so you can see clearly the areas to be trimmed.

b. The dew lap, a flap of loose skin under the chin is held between your thumb and bent pointer knuckle. This is a good all-purpose head hold. Safe, painless.

c. The dew lap and an ear, which is held with the tall man, ring and baby fingers of the hand holding the dew lap. This helps give you a little more control of the head.

d. To trim the muzzle and the side of the face turn the dog sideways. Make a V with your thumb and fingers and place them over the bridge of the nose and wrap around muzzle with two or more fingers on the underside of the jaw bone. This is another safe, firm, but gentle way to hold the head still while trimming. It also covers most of the eyes so the dog can`t anticipate your moves. When the dog goes to move you can feel it and quickly check it and say **No,** pause, then say **Hold.** When the dog complies praise him. This hold also controls biters while you trim their faces, as you have the bottom jaw under control.

Finally, snub nosed dogs also have protruding eyes and pull back because you are too close to them. Always come down the nose, stretching the nose skin backwards up the head with your free hand to allow a smooth swipe in this tight area with the clippers. Clip from the top of the head down the sides of the face working your way around the eye, gently moving the bottom eyelid over the eye as you clip under the eye. Only when the dog is comfortable with you working around their face will he let you come at him from the front to scissor trim. Go slowly and carefully and confidently in the area. I have had dogs come into my salon that have been injured by another groomer and are almost violent in their face pulling. With patience and retraining they end up resting their face in the palm of my hand, close their eyes and let me clean, tidy, clip, and trim their faces without moving. When a dog does this they have total trust in you. **Retraining, properly handling the dog and equipment are paramount in these cases.**

Snorters

These dogs know how to aim their schnookie nose mucus right into your eyes, face and mouth. This to me is as rude as a dog peeing on you, which thankfully hasn`t ever happened to me. I make note of snorters in their files and redirect their faces to the side by trimming one half of their face then the other half. I do not allow them the opportunity to face me full on. I do have a client that can flare his nostril and snort sideways at me. For this sassy guy I turn him sideways and lower the table to belly height which puts his nose at my mid chest and in a neutral firing range. Dogs are smart, you have to be smarter.

Fixed Stance

These dogs are get on your table and don`t move from one position. The have to look in the mirror, out the window, at the other dogs or their owner. They will cooperate in all of the grooming session but have to face one way. Let them, work around the table on them and you`ll be done in no time. For the dog that keeps turning away from you as you work on him, retrain him firmly with stand and stay or hold and stay. Some will be stubborn but patience and persistence will be on your side of victory.

Puppies

Puppies are very active and will need a double lanyard to keep them safe on the table. They are young and that activity will only last so long and then they suddenly tire out. To help calm the puppy down, place a drop of lavender oil on all four sides of the towel on the table. The lavender will relax the puppy and he might even start to yawn. Properly introduce all the equipment as you use it on the puppy by letting him smell it and or feel the vibration of the clippers on their body, back head and legs. He will fuss but he will realize that it is not hurting him and allow you to continue without too much trouble.

Old Dogs

Old dogs are the opposite of puppies and just need the extra support of the double lanyards, plus you need to take into account that his legs are creaky and sore and can`t be lifted as high. Dry him thoroughly after bathing and put a sweater or dog coat on him till he is ready to go home.

Blind Dogs

For blind dogs always keep your voice calm even and warm, not gushy, when speaking to him. Always have physical contact with the dog. Properly introduce each piece of equipment to him before you start using it on him. Use the same routine to groom him, every time. The dog will know what to expect next and not be surprised or frightened in anyway. The dog can`t see but he can still hear and feel and smell, so work carefully and confidently with these areas.

Injured Dogs

Be aware of the injury and any limitations to movement the injury has created whether temporary or permanent. Adjust your grooming skills to accommodate the situation.

Regain Focus

To regain focus of a dog that is easily distracted or fussing and doesn`t want to pay attention, hold the head by the dew lap and blow a puff of air into his face. The dog will automatically look at you. When he does give him direction e.g.: hold, stand and stay etc. This technique is used to get the dog to focus on you and it will work every time.

Routine

Stick to the grooming routine with every dog, every time. This builds trust, cooperation, and a quicker grooming session. Both you and the dog relax because you both know what to expect. Dogs live in the moment, you must learn to work in the moment with the dogs. Relax, stay calm, stay hydrated, play relaxing music and enjoy each grooming session with each unique client because they really deserve 'that extra scratch behind the ear'.

Glamour Shots

That Extra Scratch Behind the Ear Renaissance grooming

That Extra Scratch Behind the Ear Renaissance grooming

That Extra Scratch Behind the Ear Renaissance grooming

Glamour Shots

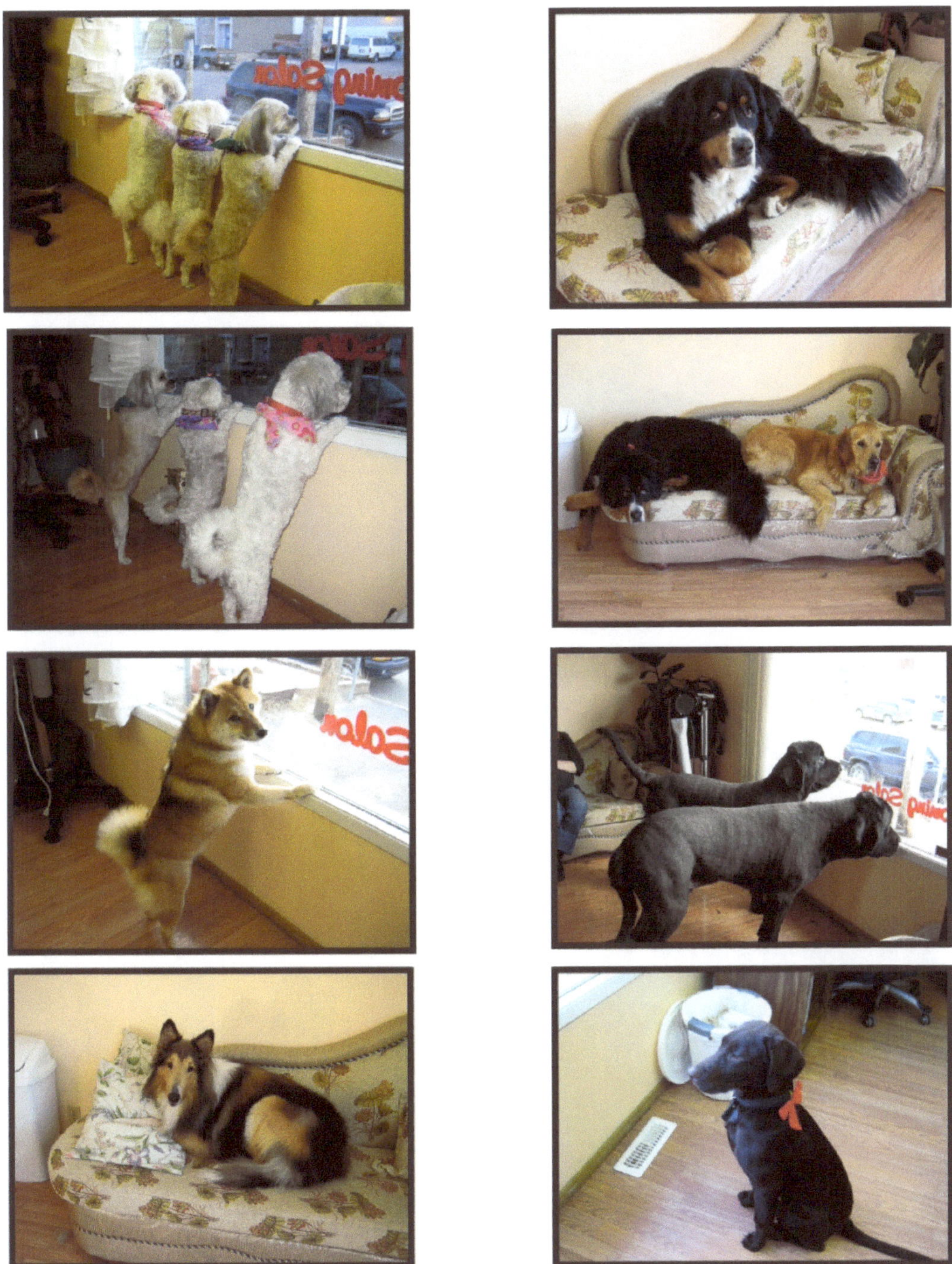

That Extra Scratch Behind the Ear Renaissance grooming

Glamour Shots

That Extra Scratch Behind the Ear Renaissance grooming

Glamour Shots

That Extra Scratch Behind the Ear Renaissance grooming

That Extra Scratch Behind the Ear Renaissance grooming

That Extra Scratch Behind the Ear Renaissance grooming

Glamour Shots

That Extra Scratch Behind the Ear Renaissance grooming

www.ingramcontent.com/pod-product-compliance
Lightning Source LLC
LaVergne TN
LVHW070134110826
845147LV00002B/249

* 9 7 8 0 9 9 5 2 2 7 8 1 1 *